P9-DUA-050

INSTANT DECORATING

Innovative interiors with impact—
100 sensational effects that you can achieve
in a weekend

INSTANT DECORATING

INNOVATIVE INTERIORS WITH IMPACT—
100 SENSATIONAL EFFECTS THAT YOU CAN ACHIEVE
IN A WEEKEND

STEWART AND SALLY WALTON

LORENZ BOOKS
NEW YORK • LONDON • SYDNEY • BATH

This edition first published in 1997 by Lorenz Books
27 West 20th Street, New York, NY 10011

LORENZ BOOKS are available for bulk purchase for sales promotion and for premium
use. For details, write or call the sales director: Lorenz Books
27 West 20th Street, New York, NY 10011; (800) 354-9657

© Anness Publishing Limited 1997

Lorenz Books is an imprint of
Anness Publishing Limited

All rights reserved. No part of this publication may be reproduced, stored in a retrieval system, or
transmitted in any way or by any means, electronic, mechanical, photocopying, recording or
otherwise, without the prior written permission of the copyright holder.

ISBN 1 85967 453 4

Publisher: Joanna Lorenz
Senior Editors: Lindsay Porter, Clare Nicholson
Photographer: Graham Rae
Stylists: Catherine Tully, Judy Smith, Andrea Spencer, Diana Civil
Designer: Simon Wilder

Printed and bound in Spain
by Artes Gráficas Toledo, S.A.
D.L.TO: 1317-1997

1 3 5 7 9 10 8 6 4 2

CONTENTS

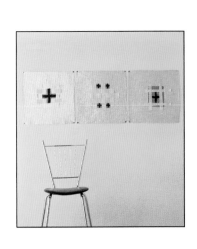

Windows

$\mathscr{I}$NTRODUCTION

Above: There is no need to hide blankets away in the bedroom; here, they have been transformed into a rich and colorful window treatment which perfectly complements the simple furnishings in this living room.

BASEMENT, BALCONY, OR BEDROOM—whatever the style of your home and effect you're looking to achieve, you're certain to find something here to revolutionize your windows. So, if you thought you had no choice but plastic curtain hooks and tracks, read on! All you have to do is invest in a staple gun and some inexpensive fittings and fixings, and follow our simple step-by-step instructions, to make your windows the fabulous focal point of each room. You will never look in curtain departments again once you have been shown our instant window makeovers and realize how easy it is to create stunning and dramatic effects. The ideas in this book will carry you away from traditional methods and old-fashioned styles toward the freshness and freedom of experimental window dressing. Many of our projects were inspired by looking at familiar materials in a new light, such as using grass beach mats for blinds or tartan wool rugs to make an imposing curtain. There are all kinds of materials that can make a leap from their everyday practical uses to highly original ones. This chapter contains projects to suit every taste and every budget, including quick, stylish ideas for tie-backs, hanging treatments and color schemes and simple effects created by draping, tying, stapling, buttoning, hanging, clipping and gluing all kinds of fabrics. You will probably come up with your own ideas and variations on our themes, too. So, armed with this innovative book, take a fresh look at the windows around your home and have lots of fun transforming them to reflect your personality. The real beauty of our quick and inexpensive window dressing ideas is that, if you happen to change your mind at a later date, you can simply change the window dressing, too.

Below left: A blank canvas becomes a work of art in this imposing project, which is ideally suited to a room with a high ceiling.

Below right: Transparent beads sparkle like jewels in the light from even a small window. As well as adding brightness, the tall shape of the bead curtain helps to elongate the natural focal point of the room.

ℰGYPTIAN DREAM

A PAIR OF COTTON SHEETS makes the most wonderful drapes, and all the seams are perfectly finished. The bigger the sheets, the more luxurious and elegant the window will look—drapes should always be generous. Wooden pegs can be wedged into a piece of old wooden floorboard or driftwood—if you drill the holes at an angle, the attachment will be stronger as well as more decorative.

YOU WILL NEED

scissors

cotton tape, 2½ yards

2 flat king-size cotton sheets

needle
white sewing thread

drill

length of floorboard or
driftwood, window width
plus 6 inches either side

6 old-fashioned wooden pegs

level

plastic anchors and screws

screwdriver

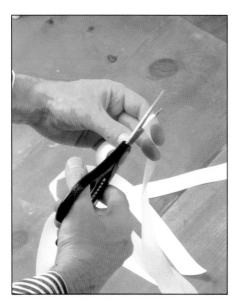

one *With scissors, cut the cotton tape into six strips of equal length.*

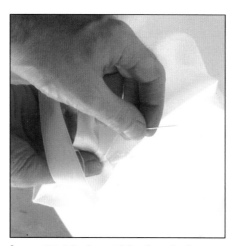

two *Divide the width of each sheet top by three and use the divisions as points to attach the tapes. Fold each tape in half and use small stitches to sew them to the top of the sheet.*

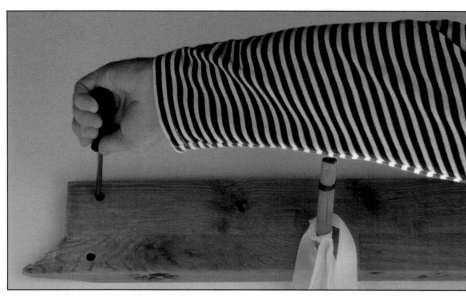

three *Drill six holes at equal distances along the floorboard and wedge in the pegs. Drill a hole at either end of the floorboard and screw it into the wall, using a level to check that it is straight and appropriate hardware to secure it.*

four *Tie the tapes securely and neatly to the pegs and arrange the drapes.*

CURTAIN CALL

THIS IS AN EXTREMELY QUICK and effective way to trim the top edge of a loop-headed curtain. Tie ribbons around the loops and hang a selection of beautiful decorations from them. Here we have used pieces of potpourri, but you can also use earrings, bells, tin stars, buttons and other decorative odds and ends. If you have a pinch-pleated or a simple gathered curtain heading, a small bow or knot with ribbon left hanging would look effective.

YOU WILL NEED

tape measure

½-inch-wide burlap
or linen ribbon or tape

dressmaker's scissors

needle and matching sewing
thread (optional)

potpourri

glue gun and glue sticks

one *Decide the appropriate length or lengths of ribbon or tape needed in relation to the drop of the curtain, so that they will look in proportion.*

two *Cut the ribbon or tape to length and cut the ends at an angle, so they look neat. If you are using a ribbon that frays, hem the ends. Select the pieces of potpourri that most complement one another. Using a glue gun, attach the pieces of potpourri to the ends of the ribbon or tape.*

three *Tie the ribbon or tape to the curtain loops. It is best not to attach them permanently, so you can change the design when you want to and take them off when you wash the curtains.*

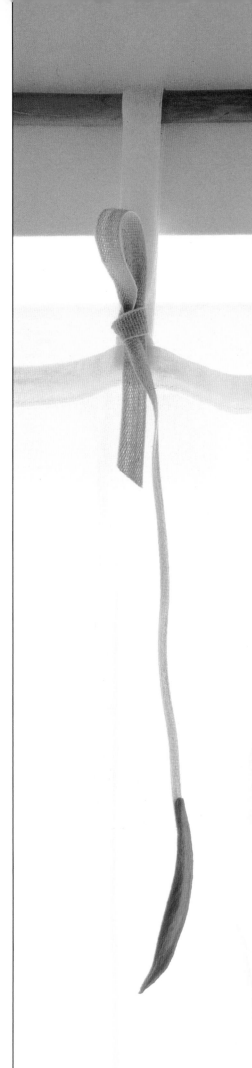

WHITE MISCHIEF

SMALL DETAILS SUCH AS the curtain clips in this project make the important difference between an obvious and an elegant solution to curtain hanging. The white muslin lawn is a generously long piece, folded in half, allowing a drop 1½ times the length of the window—it really is a very simple, yet elegant example of window dressing. Small brass curtain clips fit over the rod and catch the muslin along the fold.

YOU WILL NEED
dowel, window width
woodstain
dish cloth
drill
plastic anchors and nails
hammer
curtain clips
white muslin lawn
long thin wooden stake

one *Stain the length of dowel by shaking woodstain onto a soft cloth and rubbing the dowel with it until you achieve the desired effect.*

two *Drill two holes on either side of the window in the wall and insert the plastic anchors. Hammer in the nails.*

three *Clip the muslin along the fold, leaving an equal distance between the clips. Thread the rings onto the dowel and place the dowel over the nails.*

four *Spread the rings along the dowel so that the muslin falls in even drapes.*

five *Knot the front drop of muslin onto the end of the stake and prop this across the window.*

SHELL TIE-BACKS

CURTAIN TIE-BACKS can be made in a tremendously wide range of styles so you can use them to create whatever decorative effect you like. Though we normally think of a simple braid or tassel, tie-backs can be decorated to make them a focal point in any room. Here, a fishing net was festooned with different types and sizes of shells. You could wire a mass of very small shells onto the net or even edge the curtain with a widely spaced line of matching shells.

YOU WILL NEED
fishing net

shells

fine wire

wire cutters

glue gun and glue sticks
or electric drill, with very
fine drill bit

string (optional)

one *Take the fishing net and arrange it in graceful folds. Gather a mass of shells and see how they look best when arranged on the net. Cut lengths of fine wire. These can then be glued to the back of the shells so that they can be wired onto the net.*

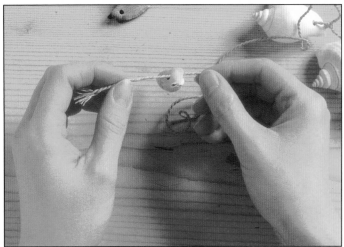

two *Alternatively, drill holes in the shells. Thread string through the holes for attaching to the net.*

three *Attach the shells to the fishing net. Make another tie-back in the same way. Loop the tie-backs around the curtains and onto the wall.*

CRYSTAL TIES

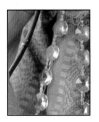

TIE AN EXQUISITE SILK curtain with crystal drops for an elegant look. The use of a very rough burlap tassel, bound loosely and casually, makes this interesting and unusual. The crystal drops were bought at an antique shop; search around for interesting examples. Or, use crystal drops from a bead store or colored stones from earrings or a cheap necklace, all of which will look equally lovely.

YOU WILL NEED
burlap tassel tie-back

scissors

crystal chandelier drops

gold beading wire or very
fine gold string

wire cutters

one *You need only one tassel tie-back for two curtains. Split the tassel in half, then unravel the rope. Re-bind the tassel to make it look less formal.*

two *Thread the crystal drops onto gold wire or fine string to make several strands of various lengths.*

three *Fasten the lengths of crystal drops onto the tie-backs. Some will simply hook on; others should be wired. Loop the tie-backs around the curtains and onto the wall.*

BIJOU BOUDOIR

BALLROOM DANCERS, punk rockers, brides and prima ballerinas all love it—netting has that special star quality that windows sometimes need. You can cut, pleat, layer, scrunch and bunch it—there is nothing to sew, and it is so light that many filmy lengths can hang from a single strand of plastic-coated sprung wire.

Netting comes in a wide variety of colors, and the idea from this project could easily be translated into a stunning party window in dramatic purple or scarlet and black. Tie the lengths of netting back with feather boas, strings of pearls or even kitschy diamanté dog collars to make the most glamorous window this side of Cannes.

YOU WILL NEED

pliers

4 eyelet hooks

2 lengths of plastic-coated sprung wire, window width

4 yards each pink and white netting (tulle)

scissors

fine wire

feather boa

fake-pearl strands

one *Screw in an eyelet hook at the same height on either side of the window recess.*

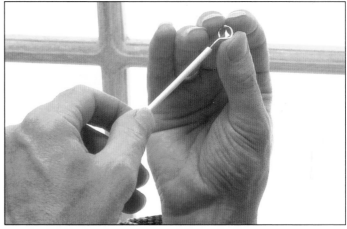

two *Loop the eyelet on the wire through the hooks and stretch the wire taut across the window.*

three *Repeat the process, positioning the second wire about 3 inches in front of the first (of course, this distance will be dictated by the depth of your window recess).*

four *Cut the netting in half. Feed half the length of the pink netting over the back wire. Set aside the rest of the pink netting.*

five *Feed the length of the white netting over the back wire, next to the pink netting. Pull both lengths of netting into shape, making a double layer with each.*

six *Hang the other layer of pink netting over the front wire, trimming if required.*

seven *Cut out a large circle of pink netting to make the valance, and fold this over the front wire to create a semi-circle.*

eight *Cut long strips of netting and scrunch them into rosettes. Tuck them between the wires. You will find that the netting is very easy to scrunch into good shapes. Pleat the semi-circular valance, adding folds and creases along the wire as you go.*

nine *Make big white rosettes to go into the corners by scrunching up the white netting. Tuck them into the wire to secure them, then smooth them out to make a pleasing shape.*

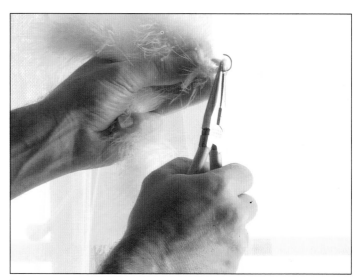

ten *Twist the fine wire into connecting rings and use them to attach the feather boa along the curve of the netting valance.*

eleven *Drape the strands of fake pearls from the center of the front wire and tie up the ends.*

Right: One of the great advantages of netting is that it is easy to handle, and is quite forgiving. If you don't like the first shape you have made, smooth it out and scrunch it up again. These rosettes are simply tucked between the front and back.

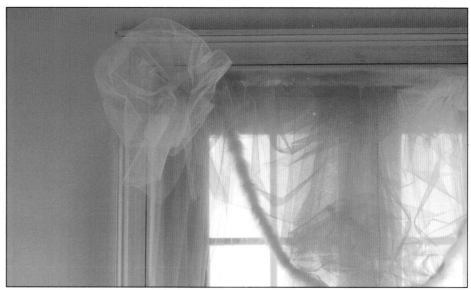

RAINBOWS

THIS REALLY MUST BE THE QUICKEST, cheapest and brightest way to deal with a bare kitchen window. It would also work well in a hallway or on a small staircase window. All you need to do is buy an insect blind—a stretch of door-length, multicolored plastic strips. Then, screw two cup hooks either side of the window frame to hold the blind, and get your scissors out for a trim. The one in this project is V-shaped, but zigzags, rippling waves or even asymmetrical designs are equally possible.

YOU WILL NEED

wooden rod

2 cup hooks

ruler

pencil

door-size insect blind

scissors

one *Place the rod along the top of the window and position the cup hooks so that the strips will hang over the whole width of the window.*

two *Measure the windowsill to find the center and make a small mark. This is where the blind will touch.*

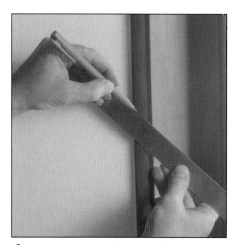

three *Place the ruler on a slant between the mark and the point you want the side drop to reach. Measure and mark the same point on the other side of the window frame.*

four *Hang the insect blind on the rod and position it on the hooks, then hold the ruler up against it, between the two pencil marks. Cut the strips along the top of the ruler.*

No-PROBLEM LINKS

WHAT LENGTHS WILL YOU GO TO for a bargain? If you find the fabric of your dreams in the remnant bin, but it's just a bit too short for your window, it's no longer a problem. Use curtain rings to connect the different lengths of fabric you have found—you can use as many as you need for the drop. Nobody will ever suspect that the linked effect was anything other than a deliberate design decision.

YOU WILL NEED

drill

metal curtain rod and attachment hardware

level

plastic anchors and screws

screwdriver

assorted lengths of fabric remnants

iron-on hem tape

iron

needle and matching sewing thread

split curtain rings

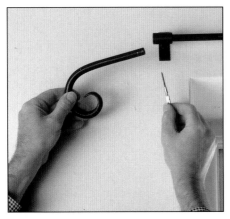

one *Attach the rod hardware above the window. Check with a level before you screw it to the wall. Assemble the curtain rod and hardware.*

‹ two *Hem all the rough edges of the fabric, either with hem tape or by hand. Sew small split rings along the top edge of the curtain to link into the rod rings. Sew rings in the same positions along the bottom of the first piece of fabric.*

three *Line the curtain up with the next piece of fabric and mark the positions for attaching the rings. Make sure they line up exactly with the first curtain if you have a geometric or striped pattern. Sew the rings to the second piece of fabric along the whole width, then hang in place.*

Above: The curtains can be linked with split rings, single rings or interconnecting rings, like these.

RIBBONS AND LACE

MAKE THE MOST OF A BEAUTIFUL PIECE of sari fabric or a superb lace panel by displaying it in a window so that the light shines through. A few hand-stitched lengths of ribbon will let you tie back the fabric to reveal as much or as little of the window and the view as you like.

As the main fabric is very light and translucent, hang a length of white muslin behind it for extra privacy.

YOU WILL NEED

muslin, 1½ x window width

iron-on hem tape

iron

white fabric tape

thread

dowel, window width

2 cup hooks

scissors

white or cream linen or satin ribbon

sari fabric or antique lace panel

one *Finish the hems on the muslin with iron-on hem tape, then sew white fabric tape along the top to tie the muslin to the dowel. Screw the hooks into the window frame and hang up the dowel. Tie the muslin onto the dowel.*

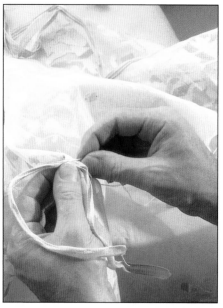

two *Cut the ribbon into eight 10-inch lengths and stitch four along the top edge of the sari fabric or lace panel. Stitch the others at intervals along the sides—their positions will depend on the size of the panel and the parts that you want to show off. You can also hide any defects when you tie them up in this way.* ❯

three *Tie the top ribbons to the dowel using simple bows. Arrange them along the dowel so that the fabric drapes over the window in the most appealing way.*

four *Tie up sections of the panel using the side ribbons. Experiment with combinations, standing back from the window to check your adjustments until you are happy with them.*

WIRED-UP WINDOW

THIS IS A QUIRKY PROJECT for people who see the window as a frame to be filled, but not necessarily frilled. A selection of crisp Irish linen dish towels, linen scrim window cloths, dusters and oven mitts are arranged on a wire framework of tracks and hangers for a practical and stylish window treatment in the kitchen. Yachting supply stores sell good wire with all kinds of interesting odds and ends for fastening and tightening up. Follow the steps here for an explanation of how to use them and ensure that everything connects securely.

Look at this window treatment as a movable feast and re-position the key elements every now and again for a new design at no extra cost.

YOU WILL NEED

rigging wire, 2 x window width; 1 x ½ window length, plus 12 inches

both attached and adjustable rigging wire grips and thimbles

hammer

pliers

2 deck eyes with pulleys

2 attached deck eyes

awl

rigging screw (tension adjuster)

connecting rings (key-ring style), various sizes

wire coat hangers

selection of dish towels, dusters, and oven mitts

‹ one *To make the rigging, thread the rigging wire through the attached wire grip to form a loop with the end.*

two *Place the thimble inside the loop and pull the wire tight, so it fits snugly around the thimble. Place it on a hard surface and hammer the wire grip closed.*

three *Loosen the screw on the adjustable wire grip and thimble and thread the other end of the wire through. Tighten the screw to hold the wire firmly in place.*

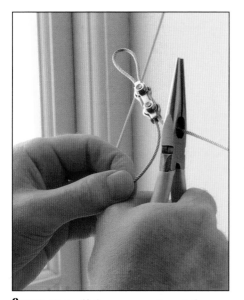

four *Cut off the excess wire at the point where it enters the thimble.*

five *Loop the thimble fitting over a deck eye, then hold it in position to the window frame while you use an awl to make holes for the screws. Screw the deck eye securely into the window frame.*

six *Thread the wire through one of the pulleys and screw this pulley into the window frame opposite the first attachment.*

seven *Thread the wire through the second pulley and screw this pulley into the window frame halfway down the side of the window.*

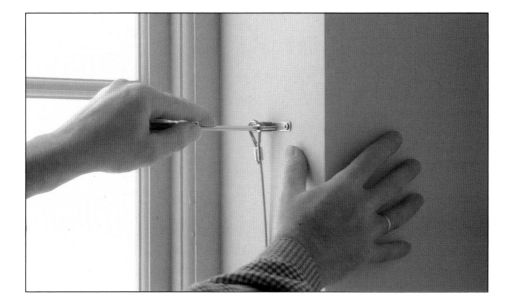

eight *Attach a thimble to the end of the shorter length of wire. Loop this through a deck eye and screw it into the frame halfway down the side of the window—opposite the last pulley.*

CONTINUED OVER ➤

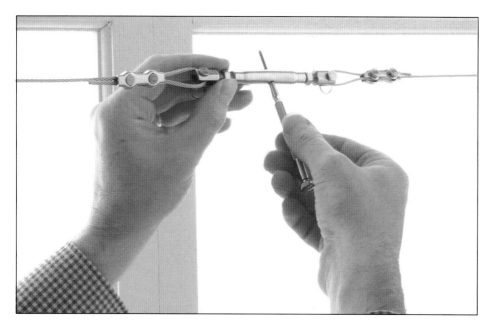

nine *Attach an adjustable wire grip so that it can join onto each end of the rigging screw. Because of the nature of a rigging screw, you will be able to make minor adjustments to centralize it, but aim to cut the wire as accurately as possible to begin with. Twist the rigging screw to increase the tension.*

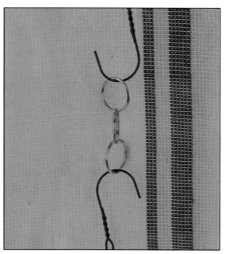

ten *To assemble the arrangement, use connecting rings to link the wire coat hangers together.*

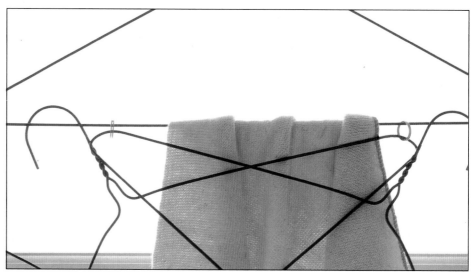

eleven *You could also make up "cat's cradle" shapes by interlinking hangers. Always reinforce the links with rings to make them more secure.*

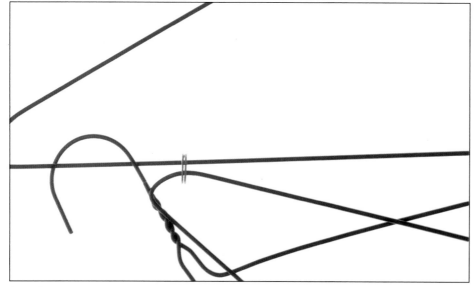

twelve *To make additional variations of the linked coat hangers, experiment with them until you are pleased with the arrangement.*

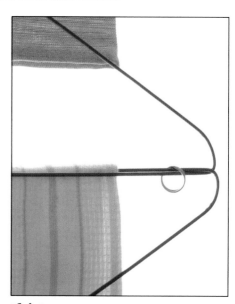

thirteen *Finally, iron the dish towels and fold them over the hangers.*

AFRICAN DAYS

KENYAN CLOTHS ARE GORGEOUSLY rich and vibrant. The patterns and colors are bold and brilliant, and there is no need to hem, stitch or gather them. Just run a clothesline across the window and pin the cloth onto it—use color coordinated clothespins and line to pull this easy and exotic window treatment together.

You won't be able to draw this curtain, but keep an extra clothespin or two handy so you can use them to hold the cloth back and let the outdoors in—even on a rainy day!

YOU WILL NEED

2 cup hooks or eyelets

plastic-coated clothesline

multicolored plastic clothespins

African cloth panel

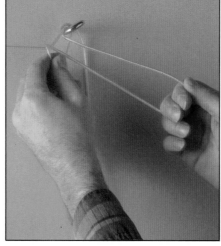

one *Screw the hooks into the wall (or window frame) at an equal distance from the window.*

two *Loop the clothesline around the hooks and tie a knot.*

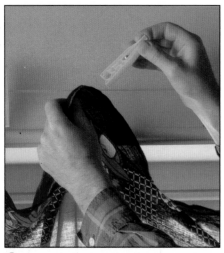

three *Clothespin the cloth to the line, gathering it up a bit for the first and last pins to add weight around the edges.*

four *Bundle up the excess line on one side and tie it in a knot. Let this hang down instead of cutting it off.*

ROBINSON CRUSOE BLINDS

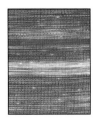

THIS REALLY MUST BE one of the cheapest, simplest, yet most effective blind solutions ever: It involves two grass beach mats, three cup hooks, a length of rope and some brass paper fasteners. The beach mats are made with colored tape binding, and as they are extremely light-weight, they can be rolled up by hand and tied with rope.

Measure your window carefully—the mats are available in one width only, so they are not suitable for all types and sizes of window.

YOU WILL NEED

awl

3 cup hooks

2 grass beach mats

brass paper fasteners

rope

scissors

one *Make three holes with an awl, one on either side and one in the middle of the window recess. Screw in the cup hooks.*

two *Make a channel for the rope at the top of the blind by folding over the mat 1½ inches and securing with a row of evenly spaced paper fasteners, pushed through and folded back.*

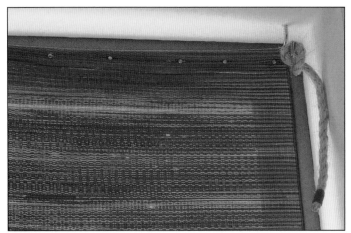

three *Knot the rope onto one of the cup hooks, leaving a tail hanging about a third of the way down the window. Thread the rope through the blind and pull it tight before knotting it onto the middle hook. Cut the rope the same length as before.*

four *Cut a length of rope twice the length of the window drop and knot it in the middle, onto the middle hook. Roll up the blind by hand and tie the two ends of this rope to hold it at the required height. Repeat this process with a second length of rope for the second blind.*

ARTIST'S STUDIO

THIS IS THE IDEAL WAY to cover a large studio window, and as canvas comes in so many sizes, you're bound to find a piece to fit your own home's window. If you have never considered the possibility of becoming a painter, then this is a good way to start—curtains can also be art.

Here, chalks were used to draw on the canvas and change the flat panel into a boldly gathered backdrop. You could use this idea as your inspiration, or you could flick colors across the canvas in Jackson Pollock style, or simply add a few minimalist squiggles. If your window receives a lot of light, you may want to suspend a builder's dust-sheet in front of the window. This will provide a lining for the main curtain.

YOU WILL NEED

canvas, 1½ x window width

chalks or acrylic paints and paintbrush

drill

4 chunky garage hooks

screwdriver

metal cleat

rope

double-sided carpet tape

brass eyelets

hammer

one *Draw, paint or print onto the canvas using whatever style or design you have chosen—the bolder the better, as the canvas will cover a large area.*

two *Fix the garage hooks securely into the wall above the window, spaced at equal intervals.*

three *Screw the cleat to the wall, about halfway down the side of the window, then wind one end of the rope around it several times.*

four *Take the long end of the rope up and through the hooks along the top.*

five *Pull the rope taut and tie it onto the end hook. Then attach the eyelets to the canvas following the manufacturer's instructions.*

six *Thread the rope through the first eyelet from behind, allowing about 6¼ inches between the hook and the eyelet. Then, leaving the same distance again, twist a loop in the rope and put it on the hook.*

seven *Take the rope down and through the back of the next eyelet, then up and over the back taut rope, which now forms a "rail" for the rope to rest on.*

eight *When you reach the end of the curtain, take the rope through the last hook.*

nine *Take the rope straight down the side of the window and tie it neatly onto the cleat.*

ten *Cut an extra length of rope and hook it over one of the top center hooks so that one length falls to the front and the other to the back of the canvas. Gather up the canvas and take hold of both ends of the rope. Tie these together in a knot and leave the ends dangling free.*

Above: The knot holding the curtain back from the window lets the light come through.

Above: Allow plenty of canvas so that it spills generously out onto the floor below the window.

Above: The knotted rope forms a decorative element in its own right.

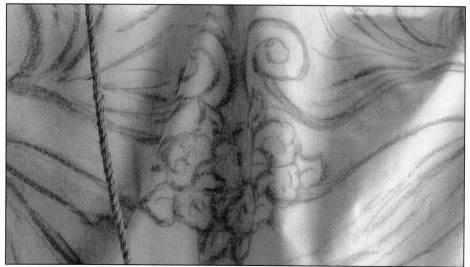

Above: The natural color of the canvas enhances the subtle colors of the design.

BUTTONED BLANKETS

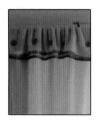

THESE BLANKETS WERE too striking to hide away in the bedroom, so they were transformed into an attractive window treatment. They're excellent at keeping out the draft and are simply rigged up on a couple of towel rods. You need a solid wall, as the blankets are heavy. The blankets are doubled over and held together with a row of large safety pins.

YOU WILL NEED

2 chrome towel rods

drill

plastic anchors and extra-long screws

screwdriver

2 colorful wool blankets

10 large colored buttons, to contrast with blanket colors

dressmaker's pins or double-sided tape

needle and thread or yarn

large safety pins or diaper pins

one *Attach the towel rods to the wall above the window by drilling holes and inserting plastic anchors. As towel rods are not long enough to cover the whole width, hang them at different heights.*

two *Fold both the blankets in half lengthwise. Drape them over the curtain rods to create a 12-inch valance, as shown. Take down the blankets. Decide upon the position of the buttons, trying them out by attaching them to the blankets with dressmaker's pins or with double-sided tape.* ❯

three *Stitch the buttons along the valance, just catching the first layer with a few stitches to secure the buttons, but without damaging the blanket.*

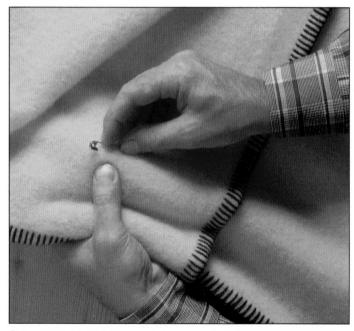

four *Pin a row of safety pins about halfway down the valance, on the underside where they won't show. Hang the blankets back in position. Re-pin carefully, so that each safety pin goes through the inside layer of the valance and the outer layer of the curtain.*

Hula-Hula

ORDINARY NYLON SHEETS that are used on the beach can be transformed into instant blinds. They come in a range of lengths with poles in pockets to divide the equal sections, just like a Roman blind, but bolder. All you have to do is saw off the extra piece of pole that would go into the sand and hang the blind on a couple of plumber's pipe fittings. A wide range of bright summer colors is available.

YOU WILL NEED

sheet of nylon, to fit window

scissors

stapler

saw

tape measure

drill

2 plastic anchors

2 plumber's pipe fittings

screwdriver

flower garlands, elastic or rope

string (optional)

one *Hold the sheet of nylon vertically against your window. If the drop is too long, then cut out the nylon mesh and make a new channel for the bottom pole. Fold over a hem, making sure the pole fits, and staple along the edge.*

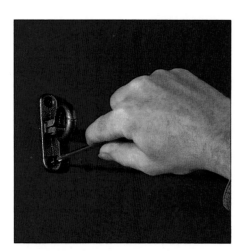

two *Saw off the excess pole, then measure the window and the top of the blind to find the position for the attachments. Drill holes and insert the plastic anchors and plumber's fittings.*

three *Hang the blind, then loop the garlands, elastic or rope between the first and last poles. If the garlands are too long, tie them in divisions with string, to shorten.*

SCOTLAND THE BRAVE

HERE IS THE PERFECT WAY to show off bright tartan wool rugs. Draped and pinned over a wooden rod, they will add a baronial touch to the plainest of windows.

Tartan has quite a masculine feel and looks good alongside old leather cases and other "practical" accessories. This window would suit a study or hallway with plain walls that would contrast with the richness and pattern of the tartan. Attach the curtain rod above the window, extending it about 12 inches on each side.

YOU WILL NEED
wooden curtain rod

level

drill

plastic anchors and screws

screwdriver

3 different colored tartan rugs

6 kilt pins

one *Attach the curtain rod according to the package instructions. Begin on the left with one corner of a rug. Take the corner over from the back and pin it about 12 inches down the rug.*

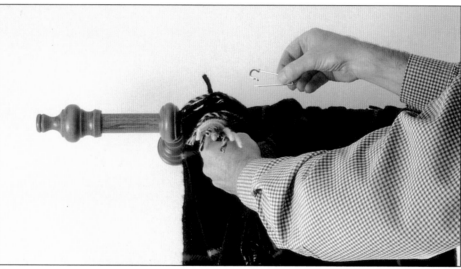

two *Drape the second rug over the rail, also on the left, but arrange it so that the drape is more or less equal at the front and back. Lift it in places and pin it onto the first rug using kilt pins.*

three *Drape the third tartan rug along the rest of the pole diagonally so that the fringed edge can be seen hanging down from the right corner. Lift sections of this rug and pin it so that it drapes by attaching it with kilt pins to the second rug.*

four *Stand back and check the effect, then use any remaining pins to hold the rugs in place, making a feature of the fringing and the pins.*

MAGIC BEADS

TRANSPARENT BEADS DON'T block out the light or keep out the draft, but when the sun catches them, they sparkle like jewels, and using them full-length on a small square window can turn a light source into something bright and magical. Beads are available in brilliant, gem-like colors, softly coordinated pastels and clear colorless textures, and each has its own unique, light-enhancing quality.

YOU WILL NEED

2 narrow wooden strips, window width, plus 3–4 inches each side

wood glue

hammer

brads or small fine nails

ruler

latex paint: black and white

paintbrush

drill

colored bead curtain, with strip to attach it and screws

screwdriver

plastic anchors and screws

level

small jeweled drawer knob

one *Make the valance by sticking one edge of a wooden strip to the long edge of the other to form a right angle. Hammer in a few brads to secure it. Divide the length into sections and paint them alternately black and white.*

two *Drill, then screw through the holes in the strip to attach the bead curtain to secure it underneath the valance.*

three *Drill, insert plastic anchors and screw the valance in place above the window. Use a level to check the position after attaching one side. Hang the lengths of beads in a pattern or at random along the strip.*

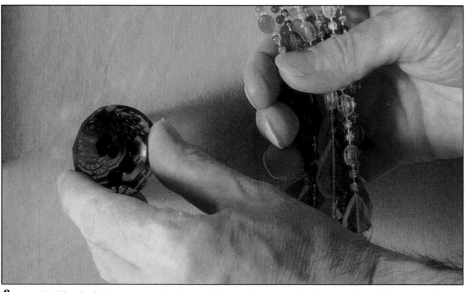

four *Drill a hole, insert a plastic anchor and screw the drawer knob into position—level with the base of the window if it is a small one, or halfway down if you have a larger window.*

MAD HATTER

IF YOU HAVE EVER felt like going right over the top with your home decorating, milliner's velvet must be the curtain choice for you. Milliner's velvet comes in gorgeous colors and is great to work with. It is backed with paper and folds into the biggest cabbage roses and most luscious drapes imaginable. A window treatment such as this is definitely not for the shy or retiring.

YOU WILL NEED

wooden strip, window width plus 4 inches on either side

level

drill

plastic anchors and screws

screwdriver

milliner's velvet in dark green and pink

scissors

staple gun

tape measure

2 or more artificial cabbages on wire stems

one *Screw the wooden strip above the window. Cut two pieces of green velvet to length and staple them to the strip in pleats, so that they meet in the middle.*

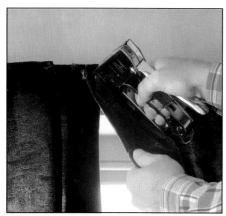

two *Cut two rectangular pieces of green velvet, roughly 1½ times the width of the window. Bunch them up and staple them across the top. Scrunch the pink velvet into three large roses and staple to the top of the valance.*

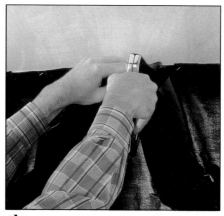

three *Staple the stems of the wire cabbages to the walls on either side of the windows. Then roll the curtains into twists and tuck behind the cabbages. Pull the cabbages in front of the curtains and staple in place.*

HANGING AROUND

MAKE THE PRETTIEST of chandelier-hangings with simple deciduous twigs such as apple or pear branches. Select a few branches with gnarled, interesting shapes and bind them together to make an eye-catching structure, then hang the finished chandelier in the center of a window, suspended from a length of gold twine. Trim the branches with sparkling trinkets such as crystal droplets and tiny pearls, all attached with the finest of gold cord. This project would also look stunning hanging from a ceiling rose or as a wall decoration.

YOU WILL NEED

2–3 apple or pear tree branches

fine gold wire

scissors

gold cord

crystal droplets

gold beading wire

small pearls

gilded decorations

one *Take the branches and move them around until they form a pretty shape. Bind the branches together at the top with fine gold wire.*

two *Attach a length of gold cord to hang the branches.*

three *Thread crystal droplets onto gold wire. Make short strings of pearls.*

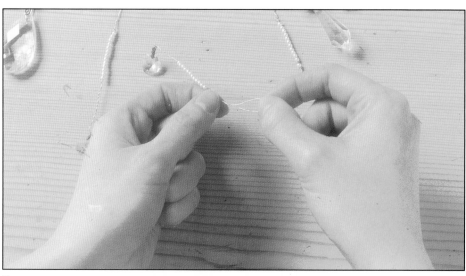

four *Wire the remaining decorations, then twist the wires to make hanging loops. Position the twig chandelier and hang on the jewels.*

WALLS AND FLOORS

$\mathscr{I}$NTRODUCTION

HOW OFTEN HAVE YOU LOOKED at your faded walls and thought about giving them a lift? How often have you looked at a jaded old carpet and wished you could afford an alternative? If lack of time and money have stopped you before, we have the answers for you. Packed with really original and innovative ideas—and without a rag roller or stippler brush in sight—these stylish projects for wall and floor decoration will provide creative inspiration, at little cost and in next to no time. Our inventive treatments go far beyond simple paint effects and are totally unique: from using photocopies for a graphic black-and-white effect, draping fabric to disguise an irregular surface, creating mosaics from broken china, or applying solid panels of color to liven up a neutral space. Applying simple paper cut outs, designing your own stencils, hanging

Below left: Geometric patterns in colored string provide a pleasingly modern and tactile solution to a plain wall. Continue the theme in your furnishings and set off the wall with a traditional wood-and-string chair.

Below right: Studs positioned at regular intervals make a refreshing change from tiles.

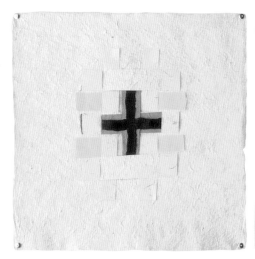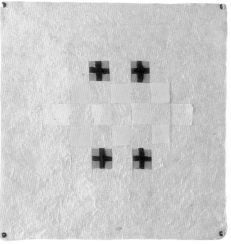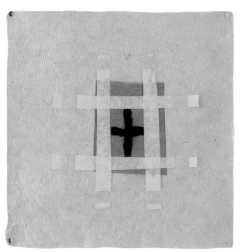

fabric—these projects will provide rich sources of ideas to help you make the most of colors and textures, and are all illustrated with the help of simple, step-by-step photographs. Floors are expensive to replace, so decisions have to be made carefully. All you need to follow our eye-catching projects is a clean, flat, level surface. If you are working on bare boards, check that they are securely attached to their joists. Sand boards down with coarse sandpaper—or hire a sanding machine—before beginning work. We have up-to-the-minute ideas for every type of floor in your house—from laying carpet tiles to resemble a board game, or creating a marbled-effect or stenciled floor.

Above: Simple cut outs made from colored and textured paper add instantly interesting detail to any wall.

Left: You don't need to spend your life savings on building up an art collection—this photocopy montage looks very impressive and won't put a dent in your pocket.

PARCHMENT PAPER ART

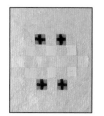

THERE IS SUCH AN INTERESTING VARIETY of textured and colored papers available at ordinary stationery stores, as well as at specialty art and craft stores, that it is easy to find the right basic ingredients to make some simple but extremely effective pictures without being skilled at painting. Choose your color combination and then make slits in the background paper through which to weave the contrasting colors. These contrasting papers don't need to be clean-cut; in fact, tearing their edges actually enhances the finished look.

YOU WILL NEED

sheets of parchment paper
sheets of colored paper
scrap paper
pencil
self-healing cutting mat
metal ruler
craft knife

one *Decide on the most interesting combination of papers. Use ordinary scrap paper to plan your design first before cutting the parchment.*

two *Draw lines on the scrap paper where you want the slits to be.*

three *Laying the paper on the cutting mat, cut these slits carefully with the craft knife.*

four *Weave paper through the slits. When you are happy with the design, rework using parchment.*

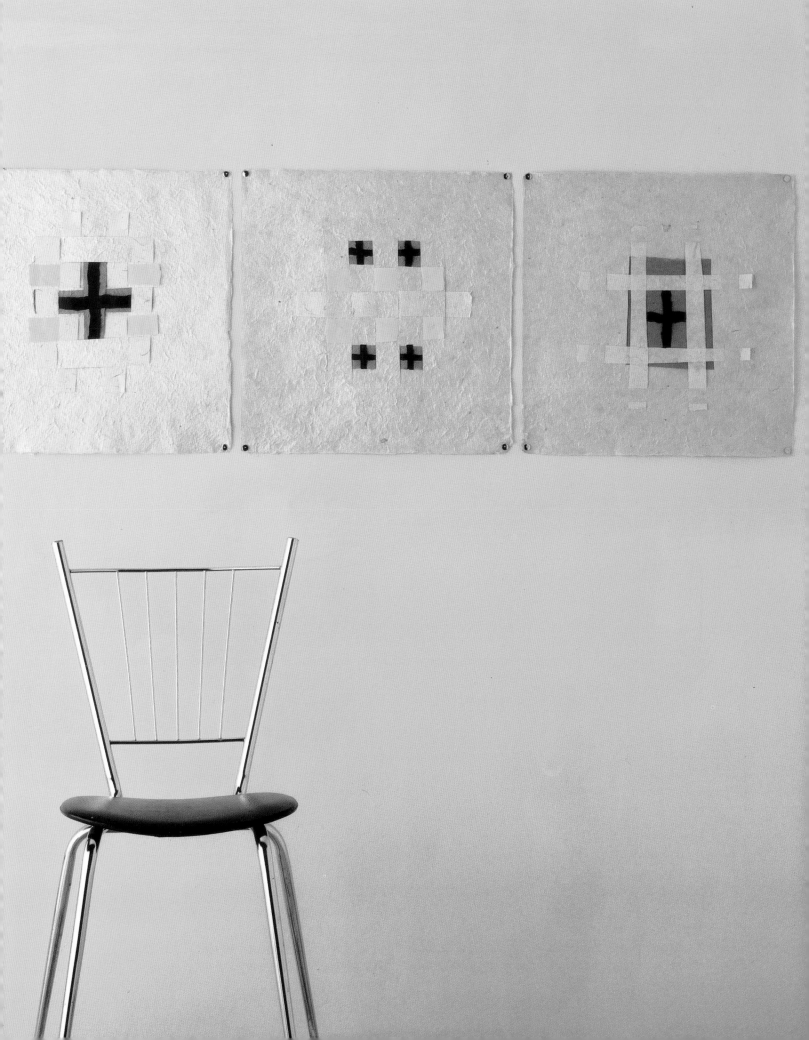

COLORED STRING

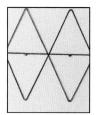

THE IDEA OF DECORATING a wall with colored string wound around tacks might evoke thoughts of nursery-school crafts, but it's surprising what wonderfully graphic patterns and eye-catching designs you can achieve with this simple technique. Set out a grid of tacks on the wall—substitute short nails if the wall won't take tacks—and then you are set to create any design you want. Just wind the string around the tacks tightly and evenly, either running the decoration across a wall from side to side or using it to make interesting borders.

YOU WILL NEED
level

straightedge

pencil

tacks

tack hammer

latex paint to match existing wall color

paintbrush

colored string

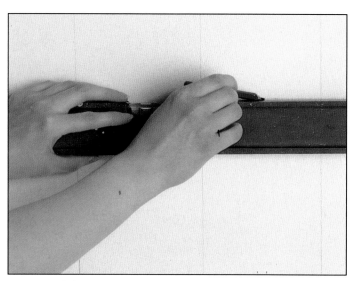

one *Lightly draw a grid on the wall, using the level, straightedge and pencil.*

two *Hammer in the tacks to the same depth at all the cross points of the grid and all around the outside edges.*

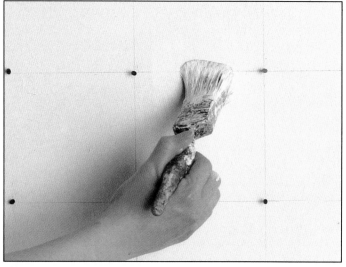

three *Paint out the pencil lines with latex paint in the existing wall color.*

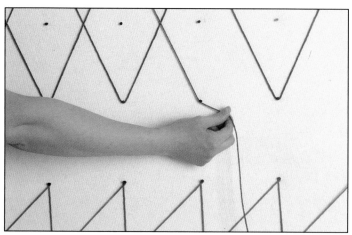

four *Arrange the string. Either buy colored string or dip plain string in colored paint to get exactly the colors you want. Wind the string tightly around the tacks, and start and finish with neat loops.*

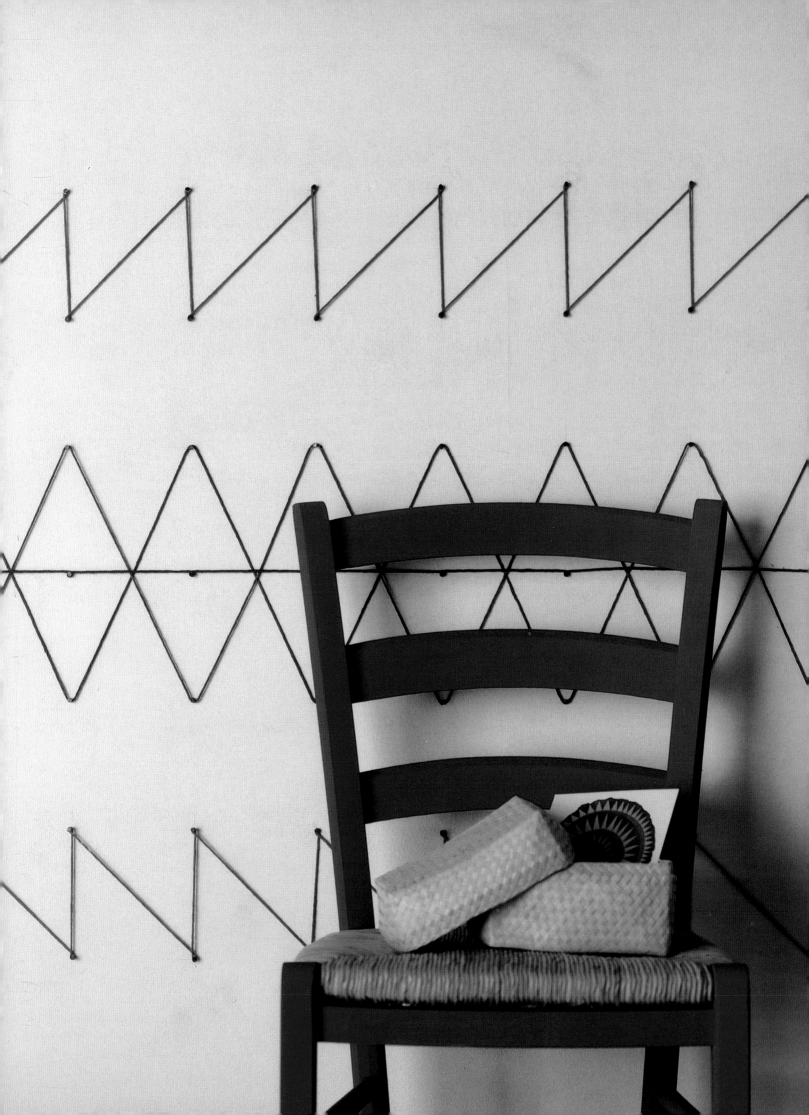

PANELS AND STAMP MOTIF

DECORATE LARGE AREAS OF a wall with these easy panels. Painting panels over a base coat quickly gives interest to large expanses of wall. It's a good idea to visually connect the panel and wall outside the panel with a simple recurring motif. This could be a strong modern shape, wavy lines or even flowers. By varying both the color of the walls and the style of the motif, you can create a wide range of different looks from the same basic treatment. Of course, you can also vary the size of the panels to fit the shape and dimensions of the room.

YOU WILL NEED

latex paint in cream, white and black

paint roller

paint-mixing tray

level

straightedge

pencil

masking tape

course brush

scrap paper

scissors

high-density foam rubber

glue

craft knife

tape measure

old plate

small roller

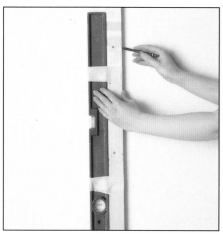

one *Give the wall a base coat of cream latex paint. Using the level and straightedge, draw the panels on the wall when it is dry.*

two *Mask off the outer edge of the panels with masking tape. Drag white latex paint over the base coat.*

three *Design the motif on paper. Stick the motif to the foam. With the craft knife, cut out the unwanted areas of the design to leave a raised stamp.*

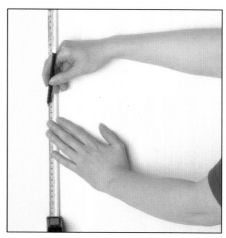

four *Decide on the spacing of the stamps and lightly mark the positions on the wall.*

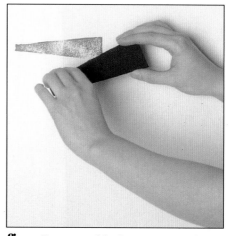

five *Put some black paint onto the plate and evenly coat the small roller. Roll the paint onto the stamp. Stamp the design in the marked positions.*

PUNCHED-TIN WALL

PUNCHED-TIN DESIGNS are surprisingly interesting and effective. They are a standard technique of folk-art interiors, but in this context, they are often kept to quite small areas. However, there's no reason why punched tin can't be used over a much larger area, where it will look much more dramatic and exciting. You will need to frame the tin in some way, so it makes sense to put it above a chair rail; it could be bordered at the top by a picture rail. Another idea would be to enclose it within moldings to form a series of matching panels on the wall.

YOU WILL NEED

scrap paper

pencil

metal file

thin tin sheet

long metal ruler

china marker

metal punch

tack hammer

wood scrap

drill, with metal and
masonry bits

level

straightedge

plastic anchors

dome-headed screws

screwdriver

clear varnish or lacquer

varnish brush

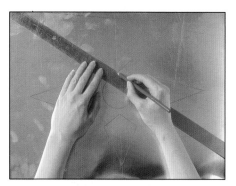

one *Design and draw the pattern to scale on paper first. Use a metal file to smooth any rough edges on the metal sheet. Draw the pattern to size on the reverse side of the metal sheet using a china marker.*

two *Practice on a spare scrap of metal to get a feel for how hard you need to punch. Punch out the pattern. Put a piece of wood behind the tin to protect your work surface. Drill holes in the corners of the metal sheet.*

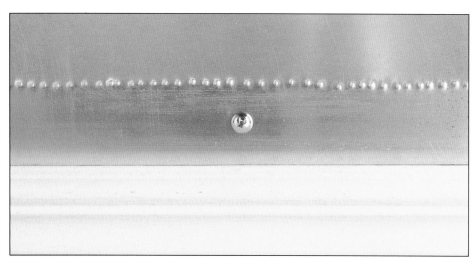

three *Using a level and straightedge, draw accurate horizontal guidelines on the wall to indicate the position of the metal sheet. Drill holes in the wall where the corners will be. Insert plastic anchors in the holes. Screw the metal sheet securely in position on the wall.*

four *Finish with a protective coat of varnish or lacquer.*

FABRIC WALL

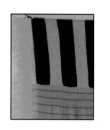

NO SPECIAL SEWING SKILLS are needed to achieve this dramatic wall treatment. Draping fabric on a wall is a good way to disguise lumps and bumps and add a lot of interest for little effort. When you have a modern fabric design, however, such as this eye-catching blanket, it may not seem appropriate to drape it on the wall in baroque folds. Instead, create a contemporary look by pulling it as taut as possible with colored string at the corners and middle of the fabric.

YOU WILL NEED

tape measure
fabric or blanket
pencil
drill, with masonry bit
plastic anchors
screw eyelets
colored string
matching strong cotton
thread

one *Measure the fabric or blanket and mark on the wall the positions for the screw eyelets, bearing in mind that you want the fabric to be pulled very taut. Drill and insert plastic anchors at the pencil marks. Screw the eyelets securely into the wall.*

two *Wrap lengths of string tightly around the corners of the fabric and around a small pinch of fabric in the middle of the two long edges.*

three *Feed the strings through the eyelets, pull them tight and secure them by looping the string back on itself. Bind the string with cotton, for a neat finish.*

BROWN PAPER PANELING

BROWN PAPER has its own characteristic color and texture, which look quite wonderful on walls. You can buy it on large rolls, which make papering under a chair rail simplicity itself. Here, the brown paper has been combined with gum arabic tape for an unusual and elegant interpretation of a classic interior look. You could also add a simple baseboard, using 2 x 1 inch timber.

YOU WILL NEED
brown paper
wallpaper paste
pasting brush
plumb line
pencil
straightedge
paintbrush
gum arabic tape
level
black beading
glue gun and glue sticks

one *Stick the brown paper, matte side inward, to the wall. Use wallpaper paste, as if it were wallpaper.*

< two *Use a plumb line and straightedge to mark vertical guidelines for the stripes on the brown paper. With a paintbrush, wet the wall in a stripe the width of the gum arabic tape and stick the tape down. Make sure you cover up all the guidelines.*

three *Use a level and straightedge to draw a horizontal guideline for the under-the-chair-rail border. Stick the tape in place in the same way as before.*

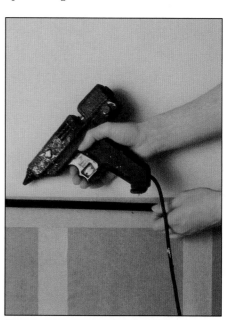

four *Attach the beading along the top of the border, using the glue gun.*

CORK-STAMPED FLOOR

THIS PRETTY STAMP has been made from seven wine bottle corks. They have been taped together in a daisy shaped bundle and the pattern shapes are cut from the surface of the cork bundle with a scalpel. Dense cork like this is a good material to carve into, as it is both soft and very smooth. With a dark woodstain, use the stamp on dust-free sanded wood or on cork tiles. Let the stamp stand and soak up the stain for ten minutes, then blot it on paper towels before you begin printing. Use the paper strips to ensure that the pattern is an even distance from the wall.

YOU WILL NEED

7 wine bottle corks
wood glue or white glue
masking tape
felt-tipped pen
scalpel
2 paper strips of equal width
dark woodstain
bowl
paper towels

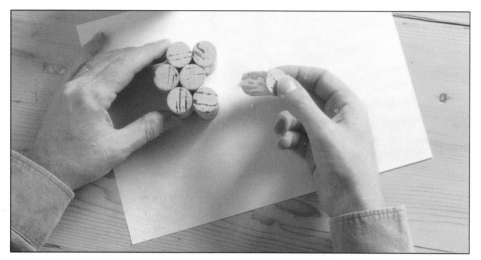

one *Glue the corks in a daisy formation, standing the ends flat on a piece of paper. This will provide a level printing surface. Bind the corks together with masking tape once the glue has become tacky.*

two *Draw the pattern onto the cork surface with a felt-tipped pen. Cut out the background pieces with a scalpel.*

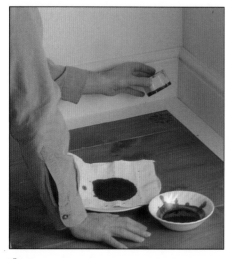

three *Start by stamping the design at each corner of the floor, placing the paper against the baseboard, as guide.*

four *Move the strips along the straight baseboard and stamp a motif about halfway between the first two. Stamp a row of evenly spaced motifs between the existing prints. Continue to stamp a border all around the room.*

FAKE ANIMAL-SKIN RUG

GIVING A NEW MEANING to the cliché of a baby on a sheep-skin rug, this fun idea could be scaled up for a full-size rug. Rather than making a classical bear-, tiger- or lion-skin rug, be more tongue-in-cheek, with shapes such as prehistoric or farm animals. Fake furs now come in a range of wonderfully bright colors, so you could take the concept even further from reality; mix up shapes and patterns.

YOU WILL NEED

large sheet of tissue paper

pencil

scissors

dressmaker's pins

fake-fur fabric

thick felt

pinking shears

yard stick or tape measure

iron-on hemming tape
and iron, sewing
machine or needle and
matching thread

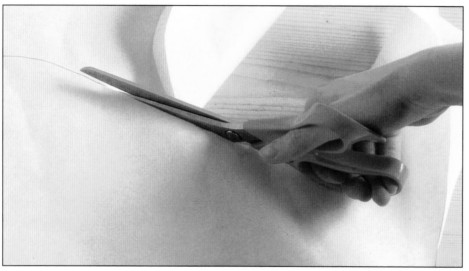

one *Draw a line down the middle of the paper, then draw half the bear shape on one side. Fold in half along the line and cut out the shape.*

two *Enlarge the paper pattern to size, then pin it to your fur fabric.*

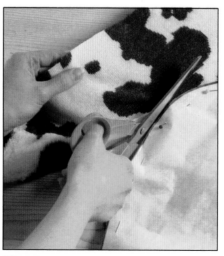

three *Cut out your shape and then cut the shape out again from the felt, using pinking shears. Include a 2½-inch allowance all around.*

four *Stick the wrong side of the fur shape to the right side of the felt shape with the hemming tape, or machine or slip-stitch the two fabrics together.*

FAUX-SOAPSTONE FLOOR

BLACK CORK TILES covering the whole floor in this room were too severe, but when the middle section of the room was treated to this wonderful soapstone effect, they became an important part of the overall grand gesture. The cork tiles in the center were replaced with a large piece of fiberboard, to which a maze pattern was applied. This could simply have been painted on plywood or fiberboard as a two-dimensional effect, but here the surface has been enhanced by routing the maze pattern (take it to a local carpenter; routing really isn't for the inexperienced) and then painted to create a soapstone effect. You could also imitate slate, by using a wave design and the black leading that was used in the nineteenth century for cleaning cast-iron fireplaces and grates (available at specialty stores). Sand or prepare your floor before beginning.

YOU WILL NEED

paper

pencil

sheet of medium density fiberboard

plastic wood or wood filler, if necessary

fine-grade sandpaper

matte latex paint: white, dark gray and medium gray

paintbrushes

wax candle

scraper

soft brush

matte varnish

one *For a new floor, plan your design on paper, using this picture as a guide. Draw it onto the sheet of fiberboard. Take it to a carpenter to be routed and ask him or her to attach it in place on your floor. For an existing floor, draw the maze on the floor directly and ask a carpenter to do the routing in situ.*

two *Fill in any mistakes or flaws with plastic wood or wood filler, following the manufacturer's instructions. Don't try to achieve a perfectly flush surface at this stage. Let dry.*

three *When dry, gently sand until you have a level surface.*

four *Paint the whole surface white and let it dry.*

five *Paint over the whole surface of the floor in dark gray.*

six *Using a candle, apply a generous coating of wax with circular movements to the surface of the floor.*

seven *Take off most of the candle wax, using a scraper.*

eight *Follow this with a coat of medium gray latex paint.*

CONTINUED OVER ➤

nine *Apply another coat of wax. Take off the wax with the scraper.*

ten *Apply white paint with a dry soft brush, to soften the whole effect. Seal with matte varnish. If you are surrounding the fiberboard with cork tiles, lay them at the end and make sure they meet neatly at the edges.*

RUBBER MATS

AVAILABLE AT RUBBER MANUFACTURERS, this safety matting is valued for its non-slip and protective qualities, and since it is waterproof, it is particularly useful in, say, a bathroom. Rubber matting doesn't fray when cut and will happily absorb any lumps or strange seams in a floor. Attach it in place using a rubber contact adhesive then clean and seal the matting with silicone spray. Make sure your floor is sanded or put in a layer of fiberboard underneath before starting.

YOU WILL NEED

2 types of rubber safety mat

tape measure

metal ruler or straightedge

craft knife

rubber floor tiles in different patterns

rubber contact adhesive

WD-40 or silicone spray

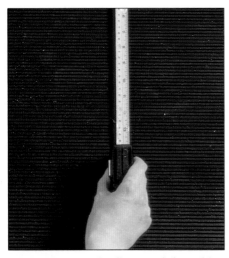

one *Measure the floor and the rubber matting and carefully trim the matting to size.*

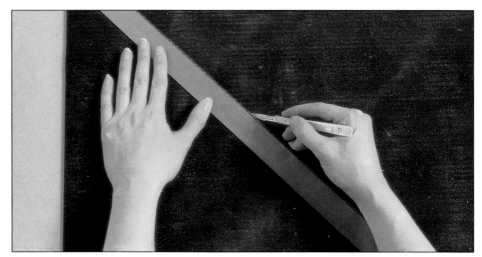

two *For the corners, cut four squares. Divide these diagonally and make four squares by placing two triangles together, with the grooves running across and top to bottom. Position these and the runners around the edge of the room.*

three *Cut pieces from the other matting to fit the central section. Cut the tiles into squares, then cut holes in the mat at regular intervals to take the squares.*

four *Secure all the pieces with rubber adhesive, applied to both surfaces. Spray with WD-40 or silicone spray.*

CHECKED FLOOR MATS

FLOOR MATS ARE EASILY available, extremely inexpensive and particularly useful, as you can usually cut them without their edges fraying. They are manufactured in many finishes, some even incorporating words, symbols or pictures, and all are produced in manageable rectangles. When these heavily textured gray polypropylene mats are arranged with the pile alternately running in different directions, an interesting checker-board effect is achieved. For a different style of room, you could create a less subtle or even thoroughly funky effect by combining two or more colors. Make sure your floor surface is smooth before starting.

YOU WILL NEED

string

white crayon or chalk

tape measure

gray polypropylene floor mats

long metal ruler or straightedge

craft knife

notched spreader

floor adhesive

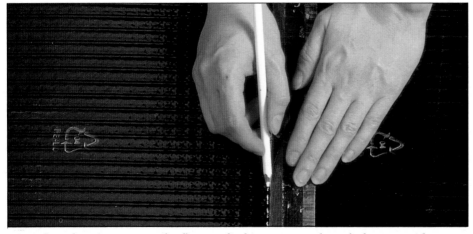

one *Stretch strings across the floor to find its center and mark the spot with a cross. If possible, link the opposite pairs of walls. Measure the floor and figure out how many floor mats you will need. Mark the cuts with a white crayon or chalk on the reverse of the floor mats.*

two *If the mats are of carpet quality, first score along the lines before cutting them with the craft knife. Then cut the mats to size.*

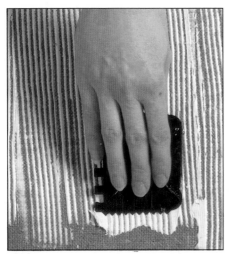

three *Using a notched spreader, apply floor adhesive to the floor.*

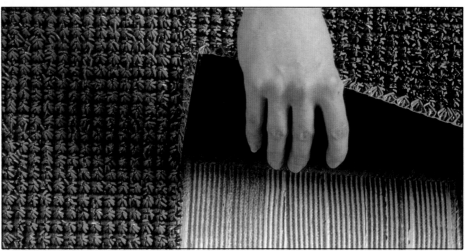

four *Starting at the center, carefully lay the mats in position, remembering that, for the checkerboard effect shown here, you need to alternate the weaves.*

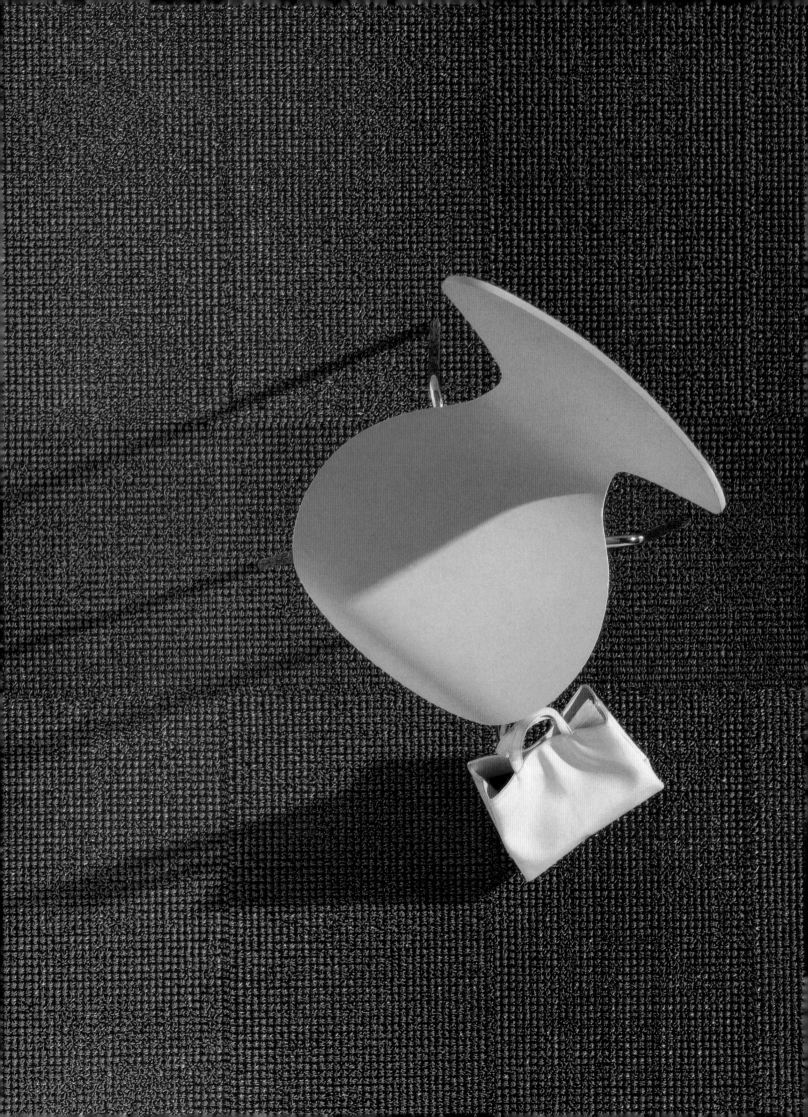

PHOTOCOPY MONTAGE

THIS EFFECT IS REMINISCENT of the wonderful painted floors of the great European palaces. Few of us can afford to commission frescoes and floor painting, but we might still aspire to a home decorated in a style fit for Marie Antoinette. Using photocopied images on a freshly prepared floor can turn these dreams into reality. Choose any theme: Our photograph shows a composition of landscapes, but architectural drawings, classical motifs such as columns, garden urns and statues, or even still lifes of fruit or vegetables could be made into successful montages. Using the same techniques, you could create a totally modern feeling using color photocopies of, say, flowers; instead of stenciling the borders, add freehand leaves and scrolls.

YOU WILL NEED

cream and green eggshell latex paint

paintbrushes

photocopied images

long metal ruler

craft knife

self-healing cutting mat

artist's watercolor or acrylic paints

gum arabic tape (optional)

pencil

masking tape

acetate sheet

bleed-proof paper (such as tracing paper)

green stencil paint

stencil brush

wallpaper paste

matte varnish

one *Starting with a well-prepared hardboard or marine-plywood floor, paint on an undercoat of cream eggshell paint, followed by a top coat. Let dry completely.*

‹ two *Experiment with images in different sizes and settle on an arrangement that looks good on your floor. Trim the images so that you are left with just the pictures.*

three *If your images are black-and-white, use watercolor or acrylic paints to put soft washes of color over the prints. You may need to stretch the paper, using gum arabic tape, depending on the quality of the paper—test a small area first.*

four *Arrange the images on the floor and draw the borders you want. Mask off the boxes for the images with masking tape. Paint between the lines of masking tape with green eggshell paint. When the paint is almost dry, gently peel off the masking tape.*

five *Make the stencil from the acetate sheet. Apply the stencil to the floor with masking tape and stipple with green paint. Glue the photocopies to the floor with wallpaper paste. Varnish the floor several times.*

STENCILED HARDBOARD

DAMAGED OR IRREGULAR FLOORS are frequently covered in hardboard and you may feel that this smooth, hard surface is especially appropriate if you have adopted a modern, minimalist approach to decorating. If you discover hardboard in mint condition, it is usually not wise to lift it, as it is probably hiding some horror below. However, with several coats of varnish, hardboard has a natural patina of its own, which is very appealing and works as a neutral background as well as a wooden floor does. Introduce additional interest by using stencils, which here mimic a fifties-style rug. The contrast of black or white works well, although the brown hardboard would suit different colors. Choose a bold, abstract pattern.

YOU WILL NEED

metal ruler or straightedge
pencil
paper
black water-based paint
paintbrushes
masking tape
self-healing cutting mat
acetate sheet
craft knife
pin
stencil brush
lint-free cloth or fine-grade
sandpaper (optional)
eraser
gloss varnish

one *Draw the border motif to the desired size on paper.*

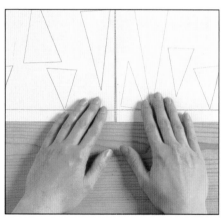

two *Photocopy the design and make sure that the pattern works, by placing several sheets together.*

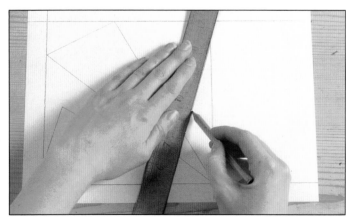

three *Make a right-angled section for the corners. Make sure it ties in neatly with the pattern on both sides.*

four *Black in the design and photocopy it. Lay the copies around the floor, to ensure that your design will fit pleasingly, and experiment until you have an effect you are happy with.*

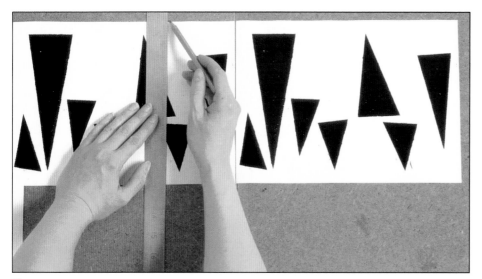

five *With pencil, mark the outer edge of your border on the floor; in the photograph, this is about 5½ inches from the edge of the room.*

six *With a pencil, draw guidelines for your border all around the room.*

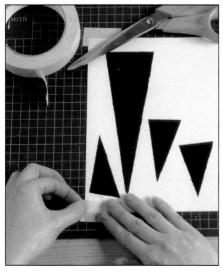

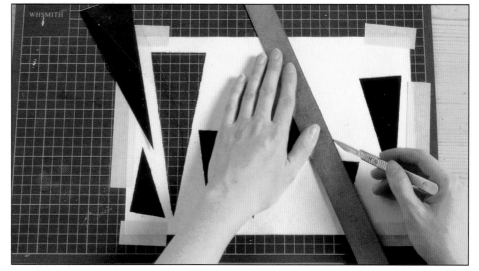

seven *With masking tape, stick one of the photocopies to the cutting mat. Tape the acetate sheet over it.*

eight *Using the metal ruler and holding the knife at an angle, carefully cut out the stencil. To help get neat, sharp corners, first make a pin prick at the corner; this also helps to prevent you from cutting too far.*

nine *With masking tape, attach the stencil to the hardboard, lining it up carefully with your guidelines.*

ten *Using a stencil brush, stipple in the neat black triangles, making sure that the paint is very dry so that it does not seep under the stencil.*

CONTINUED OVER ➤

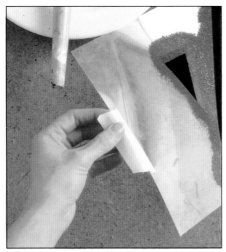

eleven *Lift up the stencil and reposition it for the next section. Remember to make sure the underside of the stencil is free of paint. If you need to mask certain areas of the stencil so that you continue the pattern when working the corners, do this with a piece of paper held firmly in place with masking tape.*

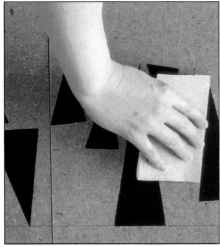

twelve *If you make a mistake or smudge the stenciling, rub it clean with a damp cloth or, if the surface is more porous, very gently sand away the paint when dry. Finally, remove the guidelines with an eraser and seal the floor with at least two coats of varnish.*

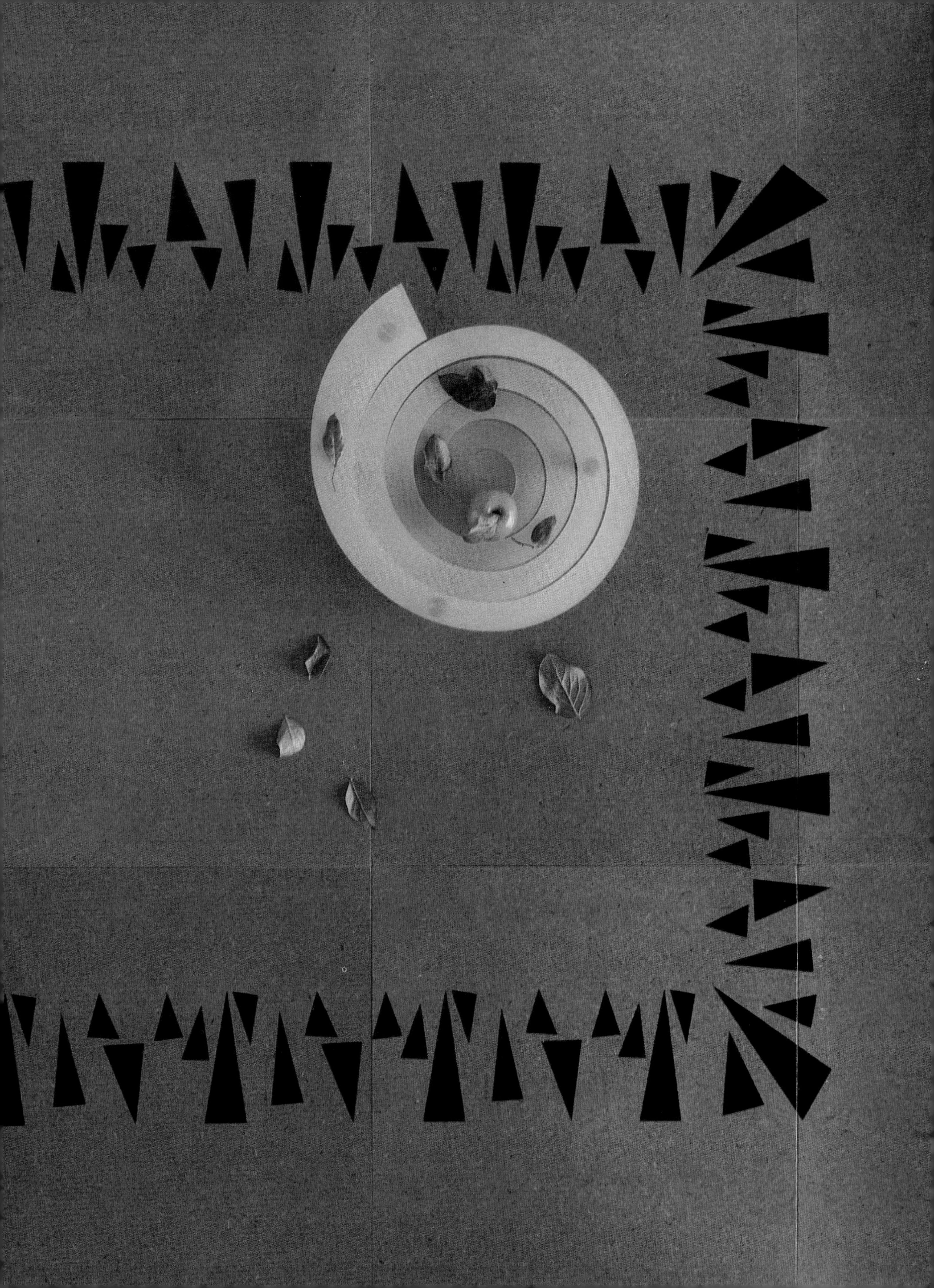

POP ART FLOOR

MUCH INSPIRATION for interior decoration is to be gleaned from the pop artists of this century, with their whimsical approach to art. These simple shapes painted on a large surface make use of the pop art conventions of sheer boldness and simplicity, with multiple repetitions of strong images rather than intricate designs. Dramatically discordant colors—orange and shocking pink in this case—are the most appropriate. This idea works best on a concrete floor.

YOU WILL NEED

white matte latex paint

paint roller

tape measure

pencil

masking tape

shocking pink, orange, red and blue matte latex paint

white glue or acrylic varnish

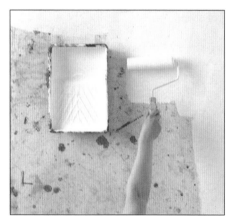

one *Give the floor two coats of white latex, to ensure that the colors of the design ring bright and true.*

two *Measure and draw out your design. Mask off the border, which needs to be crisply painted. Do the same along the outside of the star.*

three *Paint the star, then fill in the area inside the border; taping may not be necessary, as a little white space between the star and border and background makes it look as though silk-screening has been used—a technique common in pop art. Seal the floor with diluted white glue or acrylic varnish.*

STUDDED FLOOR

CREATE THE APPEARANCE of the deck of a battleship in your bathroom, with studs positioned at regular intervals across the floor and painted in battleship gray. Alternatively, you could leave the wood natural and studs unpainted. The broad silver studs used here are called "domes of silence," because they are designed to fit under chair legs to help them glide smoothly across the floor without making a noise. However, you can choose any studs, as long as they are sturdy enough to withstand the traffic on the floor and are not sharp or liable to damage shoes or furniture. Sand the floor carefully before beginning.

YOU WILL NEED

pencil
metal ruler or straightedge
studs or "domes of silence"
eraser
acrylic varnish (optional)
paintbrush (optional)
small hammer
cloth, softwood block or
carpet scrap
wood glue (optional)

one *Decide on the spacing and pattern of the studs or domes. Draw diagonal grid lines in accordance with your design and mark with a little cross where each stud is to go.*

two *Rub out all markings, except the crosses. If necessary, apply a couple of coats of acrylic varnish to the whole floor, to seal the wood.*

three *Hammer the studs in place over the crosses, using something soft to prevent damage to the studs, such as a folded cloth or softwood block. If you use "domes of silence," which have relatively shallow teeth, hammer them in only halfway to start with. Remove the domes, apply a little wood glue and then replace them and hammer them in all the way. This technique can be used on any decorative wooden floor.*

BEDS AND BEDDING

$\mathcal{I}$NTRODUCTION

Above: Fake animal prints are both postmodern and witty. If your public face is respectable and restrained, let yourself go in the privacy of the boudoir and mix and match spots and stripes as much as you please.

YOU CAN ACHIEVE INSTANT soft-furnishing style—with minimum effort—with the help of these sumptuous ideas. In the bedroom, you can let your personal style have free rein and really go to town with our instant and dramatic bed-dressing effects, and we show you how to fill the whole house with stylish, unusual and original cushions. If you don't know a four-poster from a canopy, or have always fancied a futon but didn't know quite what to put on it, then we have the answers for you. This is spontaneous and creative interior design for people with more imagination than skill and who want the opportunity to try something a little different. There are lots of ideas for dressing up basic beds, and none of the projects expect you to have advanced do-it-yourself or soft-furnishing skills—but they do promise dramatic transformations if you are willing to put in some effort. Tools and special equipment have been kept to a minimum—the only two indispensable items are a staple gun and a glue gun. These two tools

Left: Remember, we spend one third of our lives in bed, so the surroundings should be as delightful as possible. Customize your cushions and scatter them on beds, in armchairs and even on the floor to create a space that is ideal for reading, contemplating or just lounging.

provide freedom from conventional methods of construction, fixing and draping, and allow you to achieve the impossible. Bed dressing can be just what the name suggests—giving your jaded divan a new set of covers—or it can be making a headboard, hanging up drapes or even building a four-poster frame, which really isn't as daunting as it sounds. And follow our fantastic ideas for cushions to liven up a neglected sofa or armchair or to throw over your newly revamped bed. Whichever project you choose you'll have hours of fun following our clear and easy step-by-step instructions and transforming your chosen object with minimal expense and fuss.

Right: You don't have to be Scottish to appreciate this treatment. A tartan bed-head takes very little effort to make and is a perfect alternative to feminine frills. Hang your tartan from a rod to disguise a plain or uneven wall, protect the sleeper from evening drafts and provide a focal point for the room, all in one.

ℒOVELY LINENS

PRETTY UP PERFECTLY PLAIN LINENS with splashes of vibrant color. To add definition, border with strips of rickrack edging; for frilliness, buy eyelet lace and sew it onto the pillowcase. You could then weave ribbon or tapestry yarn through the lace to add color. Alternatively, look for linens that have a fine-holed edging and thread through the holes with fine tapestry yarn. To complement the edges, add tiny decorative crosses to buttons sewn onto the pillowcase. A more time-consuming, but extremely effective decoration is made by scalloping the edge of a sheet and decorating with tapestry yarn.

YOU WILL NEED

paper

pencil

cardboard

scissors

single or double white sheet

sewing machine

white sewing thread

small, sharp-pointed scissors

red tapestry yarn

tapestry needle

plain pillowcase

3 yards eyelet lace

dressmaker's pins

needle and basting thread

buttoned pillowcase, with
fine-holed decorative edge

glue gun and glue sticks

decorative red buttons

small cushion, with
frilled-edge and
center-opening cover

one *Cut out a cardboard template for the sheet edging. Draw around it, then machine satin-stitch over the line. Cut along outside the sewn line.*

two *Cut lengths of colored tapestry yarn and knot the ends. Sew the lengths of yarn through the sheet, leaving the long ends as decoration.*

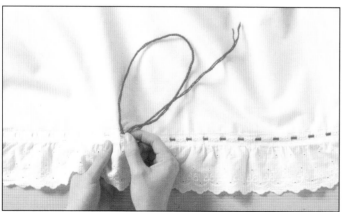

three *Edge the plain pillowcase with eyelet lace. Then use a tapestry needle to thread colored yarn through the holes in the lace. You can also use this technique to decorate pillowcases with fine-holed decorative edging.*

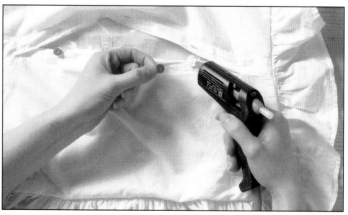

four *You can liven up plain buttons on a pillowcase by using a glue gun to apply decorative colored buttons on top. Decorate around cloth buttons by making neat cross-stitches over them with tapestry yarn.*

TRIMMED CUSHIONS

DRESS UP A PILE OF PLAIN CUSHIONS and transform the atmosphere of your bedroom in an afternoon. The embellishments used here are dressmaker's trimmings, which are available in a wide range of materials, shapes, colors and sizes. Upholstery trimmings tend to be more expensive and the range is limited, so it is well worth looking out for a dressmaking specialty store. Craft or sewing stores often carry notions and scraps, with short lengths of fringe, beading, braids and lace, which are ideal for embellishing cushions. Tie tassels and cord around the ends of a bolster cushion, for example, or embellish a plain black cushion with an unusual motif.

YOU WILL NEED

3 cushions: 2 velvet and 1 silk

fringe

needle and matching threads

pencil

compass

thin cardboard

scissors

pins

black lace and fringe

black bobble trimming

tape measure

one *For the first cushion, slip-stitch the ends of a length of fringe, so that it doesn't unravel.*

‹ two *Cut a quarter circle from thin cardboard and place it on the cushion as a guide for the curve of the fringe. Slip-stitch along the edge of the fringe using matching thread.*

three *For the second cushion, pin three or four parallel rows of black lace and fringe onto a yellow-ocher velvet cushion.*

four *Slip-stitch the trimmings in place with matching thread.*

five *For the third cushion, stitch two rows of black bobble trim onto an orange silk cushion. Pin one row, then use a tape measure to line up the second.*

VICTORIAN LACE

NOTHING LOOKS MORE ROMANTIC and feminine than a brass bed covered with snowy white, lace-trimmed bed linen. Make layers of scallops and frills on sheets, bolsters, pillows and bedcovers. Start by buying a good cotton duvet (or comforter) cover with a scalloped edge. Search second-hand stores and flea markets for lace-edged tablecloths, dressing-table runners, tray cloths and curtain panels. Look for old white cotton sheets with embroidered edges to add interest.

YOU WILL NEED

plain white bed linen

selection of lacy tablecloths, tray cloths, mats, chair backs or dressing-table runners

pins

iron

iron-on hemming tape or needle and white thread

bolster

rubber bands

white ribbon or raffia

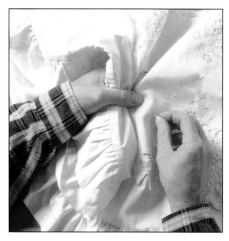

one *Select suitably sized lace additions to make central panels or corner details on the pillowcases and duvet cover. Pin them in position.*

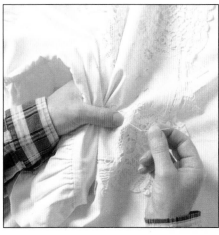

two *Use iron-on hemming tape and an iron to bond the two layers together, or slip-stitch them in place.*

three *Roll the bolster up in a lace-edged tablecloth and bunch up the ends, securing them with rubber bands. Tie ribbon or raffia over the gathered ends and drape the lace edging.*

CANOPIED BED

A SIMPLE DRAPED CANOPY is a great way to define and decorate a sleeping area without completely enclosing it. The muslin is draped over a wooden trellis. The natural rustic character of the twigs combines very well with the unfussy appearance of unbleached muslin. Muslin is inexpensive, so buy more than you need—any extra will make a pretty cascade at the end of the bed.

YOU WILL NEED

at least 12 yards
unbleached muslin

iron-on hemming tape

iron

trellis

rubber bands

twine

scissors

ceiling hook

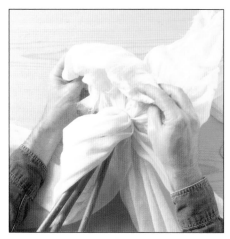

one *Turn up a hem at each end of the fabric and use iron-on hemming tape to make a neat hem. Find the middle of the fabric length and bunch and wrap the muslin around the narrow end of the trellis at this point.*

two *Pull the fabric into a pleasing shape, then secure it with rubber bands. Wind the twine to cover the rubber bands and decorate the fabric.*

three *Attach a ceiling hook centrally above the bed. Hang the trellis from it. Drape the muslin on either side of the trellis and over the bed ends.*

BEACH MAT BED

A SIMPLE FOUR-POSTER FRAME can be built to fit around an existing base and mattress. This requires only basic carpentry skills, as the timber can be cut to size when you buy it and just needs drilling and screwing together. The wood used here is basic construction timber that has been left in its natural state, but you could color it with woodstain or paint it to coordinate with the decor of the bedroom.

Grass beach mats are perfect for hanging around the four-poster, especially if your room is decorated with natural fabrics and earth colors. The loosely stitched grass mats let a soothing, soft golden light filter through and allow the air to circulate.

YOU WILL NEED

grass beach mats

package of brass paper fasteners

rough twine

scissors

odd-shaped shells, pebbles and driftwood

one *Fold one short edge of each beach mat over the top rail of the four-poster frame. Push paper fasteners through the mats just below the rail and open out the prongs. Use four fasteners along the top of each beach mat.*

two *The mats are edged with different colored tape that makes fine stripes around the bed. Arrange the mats to make the most of this striping.* ›

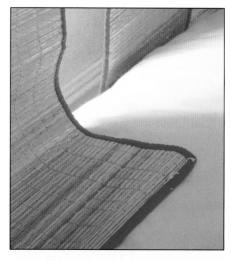

three *Decide how many blinds you want to tie up—maybe all, or just a select few. You will need about 1 yard of rough twine for each mat to be rolled up. Cut the lengths required, and tie some shells, pebbles and bits of driftwood randomly along the length and at each end of the twine.*

four *Dangle the ropes with shells and stones over the top rail and use them to tie back the rolled-up blinds.*

ROMANTIC NETTING

EVEN IF YOU HAVE NO practical need for mosquito netting, the light and airy beauty of this project makes it ideal for the bedrooms of urban romantics who dream of being in the Punjab or on the Serengeti plains. Netting like this can be bought at camping stores and comes complete with a spoked wooden coronet that opens like a fan to support it. Here, the spokes have then been decorated with dangling glass ornaments to make the netting look more exotic than utilitarian. Plain white netting is very appealing, but it can also be dyed to any pale color.

YOU WILL NEED

mosquito netting, with coronet and fixings

dangling glass ornaments and earrings

fine wire

long-nosed pliers

ceiling hook

one *Fan out the spokes of the wooden coronet and fit them into the channels of the netting.*

two *Thread assorted glass ornaments, beads and earrings onto lengths of fine wire to make decorative pendants.*

three *Thread the wire ends through the netting at the bottom of the spokes. Use long-nosed pliers to twist the ends together to secure them.*

four *Attach the ring and rope provided to the center of the coronet. Hang the net from a ceiling hook above the bed.*

BLACK-AND-WHITE PRINTS

IMAGINE BEING ABLE to decorate soft furnishings with any image or picture of your choice. There is now a special transparent gel available that enables you to transfer black-and-white or color images onto fabric. The image can then be sealed to make it resistant to wear and tear. By enlarging or reducing the images on a photocopier, you can obtain a selection of prints that will fit perfectly onto any item that you would like to decorate, such as cushions, pillows or even a quilt. You can use the same process to monogram your bed linen in royal style. However, because the image will be reversed once it is transferred, you will have to photocopy any lettering onto acetate first.

YOU WILL NEED

photocopies of chosen images

scissors

plain-colored cotton cushion cover

iron

plastic trash bag

image-transfer gel

paintbrush

soft cloth

sheet of acetate (optional)

one *Choose your images and make the required number of copies. Here, several copies of the same image are used to form a frame around the portrait.*

two *Cut away all the excess paper, leaving only the images that you want to transfer.*

three *To design the cushion cover, arrange the images on a flat surface. Experiment with spacing until you are happy with the design.*

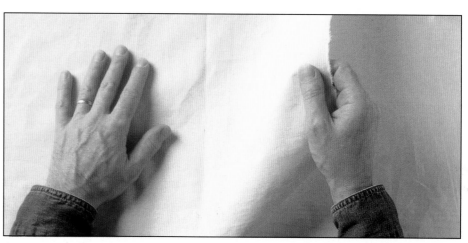

four *Pre-wash and iron the cushion cover. This is important because glazes used to stiffen fabrics may adversely affect the transfer process. Place the cover on a plastic trash bag to protect your work surface.*

five *Paint a thick layer of transfer gel onto the first photocopy, making sure that you have covered it completely.*

six *Place the image face-down in position on the cushion cover and gently rub all over the back with a soft cloth. Leave the image in position.*

seven *Repeat steps 5 and 6 with all the images, ensuring that they are positioned accurately before you make contact with the fabric. Let transfer overnight.*

eight *Soak the cloth with clean water and then use the wet cloth to saturate the photocopy paper.*

nine *Keep the cloth wet and begin to rub away the paper, working from the center outward. The images will have transferred onto the fabric. When all the paper has been removed, let the fabric dry.*

ten *Apply a final setting coat of the transfer gel to the prints and let dry completely.*

CONTINUED OVER ➤

eleven *You can use the same process to monogram your bed linen. Photocopy the initials onto a sheet of acetate. Then turn the acetate over and photocopy from the acetate onto paper to reverse. Cut out the print.*

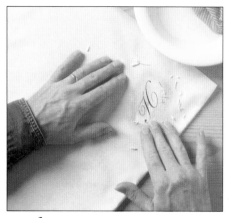

twelve *Transfer the initials as described in steps 5 to 10. The transfer process will reverse the initials once more, so that they are now the right way around.*

ANIMAL CUSHIONS

ANIMAL PRINTS HAVE NEVER BEEN more popular, and the quality of fake fur now available is truly fantastic. It is also a delight to animal-lovers and the environmentally conscious. The distinctive boldness of the cowhide print chosen here makes for great cushion covers.

This low bed is draped with lengths of silky smooth velvet tiger- and leopard-skin fabric that spill over onto the floor, adding to the tactile, languorous atmosphere. This project doesn't have to be a permanent fixture, so bring out this special bedding for wild weekends—and it may bring out the animal in you!

YOU WILL NEED

cardboard

scissors

button blanks

small pieces of black velvet

hemmed squares of cowhide print, 2 inches smaller than the cushions

black velvet cushions

needle and thread

tiger- and leopard-skin fabrics

one *Cut a circle of cardboard approximately ½ inch larger all around than the button blanks. Use the cardboard pattern to cut circles of black velvet.*

two *Cover the top of each button blank with a velvet circle, tucking in the edges so that they catch onto the spikes underneath.*

three *Press the backing firmly in place to make neatly covered black velvet buttons.*

four *Stitch a hemmed cowhide fabric square diagonally on each cushion. Sew a black button onto the center, stitching through both the cowhide print and the black velvet cushion. Arrange the tiger- and leopard-skin fabrics over the bed.*

DREAM TRELLIS

DRESS UP A PLAIN WALL behind a simple bed with a most unusual trellis headboard made from woven twigs and branches. The trellis is very lightweight and is easily set in place. Continue the theme with twig accessories, such as chairs, and complement the decor with crisply starched white sheets and pretty cushion covers.

Country garden centers are always worth a visit, because trellis-work like this is handmade, and producers often use local garden centers as outlets. Alternatively, you might like to try making a trellis yourself.

YOU WILL NEED

garden raffia

scissors

handmade twig trellis

masonry nails or
cavity wall fixtures

hammer

one *Divide the raffia into two bunches of approximately twelve strands each. Knot one end of each bunch.*

two *Braid the strands to make two braids about 4 inches long.*

three *Tie the braids onto the trellis 10 inches from each end. Attach the braids to the wall above the bed, suspending the trellis behind the bed.*

LOVE PILLOWS

MAKE SURE THE RIGHT message gets across by stenciling the word "love" on your pillows in both English and French, the archetypal language of romance. The typeface used is the graphic designer's favorite, Gill (bold), chosen for its stylish simplicity and clarity. There is no doubt what is meant here. The word has been enlarged on a photocopier to 7 inches long. You can adapt this idea for other messages that are completely personal and private, but if you have children, discretion may be a good idea. Choose colors that match your bedroom's overall scheme or that are your favorites. Fabric paints are available in a wide range of colors. Always wash and iron the fabric before stenciling to rid it of any glazes that could block the color absorption.

YOU WILL NEED

photocopied enlargement
of the words

spray adhesive

2 pieces of stencil cardboard

scalpel or craft knife

cutting mat or thick cardboard

sheet of thin cardboard

white cotton pillowcases

fabric paint

plate

stencil brush

iron

one *Enlarge the templates to the required size. Spray the backs of the photocopies with spray adhesive and stick them onto the stencil cardboard.*

two *Cut out the letters on a cutting mat. The O, A and R need ties to retain the internal letter features, so draw in "bridges" before you cut them out.*

three *Place a sheet of thin cardboard inside the pillow case, so that the color does not bleed through to the other side.*

four *Apply paint sparingly to letters. You can always build up color later, but too much paint can cause problems. When dry, seal with a hot iron.*

AEOL
MRUV

GINGHAM HEADBOARD

THIS HEADBOARD CONVERSION creates a fresh new style with added comfort. Gingham always looks crisp and clean, so you will wake up bright-eyed and ready to face the day. It is available in both small and large checked patterns and in a wide variety of both bright and pastel colors. The gingham is backed with quilter's batting. Alternatively, you could use other fabrics to create a different sort of mood—a small floral print for a feminine, country cottage decor or a vibrant primary color for a teenager's room, for example. The headboard should be rectangular in shape and can be solid or of a slatted or spindled type. Measure the width and height of the headboard, then double the height measurement so that the gingham folds in half over the top.

YOU WILL NEED

iron-on quilter's batting

tape measure

dressmaker's scissors

iron

gingham, width of the headboard x twice the height, plus seam allowance on all edges

iron-on hemming tape

needle and matching sewing thread

2 yards red ribbon

pins

one *Cut the batting to the size of the headboard. Press one end of the gingham onto the batting. The other end of the gingham will fold over the headboard back. Leave a large seam allowance all around the edge.*

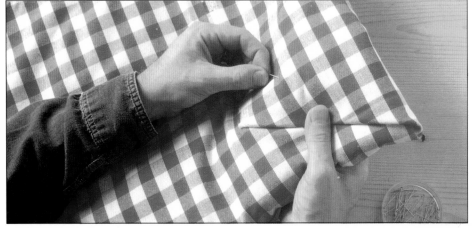

two *Fold the seams over and tuck the corners in neatly. Use iron-on hemming tape or a needle and thread to secure the edges. As the hems will be on the inside of the cover, they will not be visible.*

three *To make the ties, cut the ribbon into 16 equal lengths.*

four *Pin, then sew four ribbons, equally spaced, along the inside edges of each side of the cover. Fold the cover over the headboard and tie the ribbons in bows to finish.*

CHINTZ HEADBOARD

GIVE YOUR PADDED HEADBOARD a new lease on life with old chintz curtains. The fabric improves with age, as the colors fade and mellow delightfully, and it looks wonderful teamed with crisp white cotton, handmade quilts or plaid wool blankets in a traditional bedroom. Use the very best section of pattern for the bedhead and tuck remaining lengths under the mattress to form a valance. If you prefer a more permanent valance, you could sew pleated lengths of the same chintz fabric around the edges of a fitted sheet.

<u>YOU WILL NEED</u>

pair of floral chintz curtains
scissors
tape measure
headboard
pencil
staple gun and staples

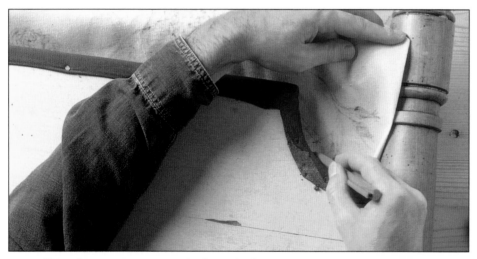

one *Trim the curtains to get rid of any thick seams, curtain tape and bulky hems. Cut a strip of curtain long enough to fold over the front and onto the back of the headboard at the sides, top and bottom. Smooth it over the front of the headboard then move to the back. Draw any curved corners onto the back of the fabric.*

two *Cut notches in the fabric right up to the drawn line, so that the fabric will fit the curve without puckering. Staple each cut strip onto the headboard.*

three *Pull down the top flap tautly and staple it onto the headboard.*

four *Pull up the bottom flap tautly and staple it in place. Staple both side edges in the same way. Cut a panel of fabric to cover all the stapled edges on the back. Turn in the edges and staple the panel flat onto the backing board.*

ENTWINED HEADBOARD

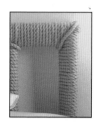

QUITE APART FROM BEING one of the most stylish looks around, rope-wrapping is a real pleasure to do. All you need is a frame, which can be a junk-shop find or a homemade structure made from construction timber. The wood is completely hidden by the coils of rope, so there is no need to prepare the surface in any way. Rope comes in many different twists and thicknesses, some more decorative than others. Some ropes are made from natural fibers and others, like the one used here, are synthetic. An advantage of synthetic rope is that the ends can be sealed by holding them over a flame to melt the fibers together.

YOU WILL NEED

rope

wooden-framed headboard

tape measure

pen

scissors or craft knife

cutting mat or thick cardboard

lighter or matches (optional)

glue gun and glue sticks

one *To calculate the length of rope needed to wrap each wooden post, first divide the height of the post by the thickness of the rope. Multiply this figure by the circumference of the post. Mark the rope at this point.*

two *Cut the lengths of rope required to wrap all the posts. If you are using synthetic rope, seal the ends by holding them briefly over a flame. Use the glue gun to stick the end of the rope to the back of the first post to be wrapped.*

three *Wrap the rope tightly around the post, keeping the coils as close together as possible. To maintain the tension, apply a few dabs of hot glue.*

four *Cut short lengths of rope to cover gaps, loose ends and blobs of glue at the intersection. Glue the ends at the back.*

five *Make sure that all the intersections are finished in the same way so that the symmetry is maintained. Finish with rope decorations.*

HAMMOCK QUILT

RECLINING IN A HAMMOCK MAY BE THE ULTIMATE relaxation, but it is really possible to lie back and enjoy the sway only if you feel completely secure. So make quite sure that your wall fittings are sturdy and properly installed and that the wall itself is strong enough to take the strain. Use strong metal garage hooks with long screws and heavy-duty plastic anchors. Once the issue of safety has been covered, you can then turn your attention to comfort and make this stylish and simple no-sew quilt to dress up your hammock and keep you cozy. The next step is simply to hop in and rock away your cares.

YOU WILL NEED
iron
2¾ yards iron-on batting
5½ yards blue fabric
2¾ yards black cotton fabric
scissors
tape measure
iron-on hemming tape
5½ yards black iron-on mending tape
pins

one *Iron the batting to one half of the wrong side of the blue fabric. Then fold the other half over so that the batting is sandwiched by the blue fabric. This will give the quilt some thickness. Next, cut the black fabric into four 5½-inch-wide strips to fit the quilt edges. Press a ½-inch hem along the long edges. Iron each strip in half to make a long doubled strip 2¼ inches wide. This will be used to border the blue cloth. Place a length of iron-on hemming tape along each edge of the blue fabric and enclose each edge with a doubled black border strip. Iron to bond the fabrics. Fold down the corners of the black edging to achieve a mitered effect. Turn the fabric over and repeat on the other side.*

two *Cut twenty-four 8-inch strips of iron-on mending tape and use the tape measure to position them on the quilt in four rows of three crosses.*

three *Pin the crosses in place, if required, then iron them in position.*

TARTAN BEDHEAD

WOOL TARTAN RUGS are real comfort blankets, tradition-ally used on winter car journeys and picnics. The two rugs used in this project are doubled over, with their folded edges meeting in the middle. To complete the Highland hunting lodge atmosphere, the rugs are hung above the bedhead from a rough-hewn "branch."

YOU WILL NEED

2 matching tartan blankets
or rugs

kilt pins

tape measure

needle

thick contrasting thread

1-inch wooden dowel
(slightly longer than the
bed width)

craft knife

fine-grade sandpaper

cloth

shellac

2 iron pipe holders
(to fit 1-inch pipe)

drill and plastic anchors

screwdriver

one *Fold each blanket in half length-wise and pin together along the folded seam. Blanket-stitch the outside edges, then stitch the blankets together along the folded edge. If you don't like sewing, hold the seams closed with three kilt pins.*

two *Start decorating the wooden dowel by roughly carving away both ends of it with a craft knife. Sand the rough edges with sandpaper. Use a cloth to rub shellac into the wood.*

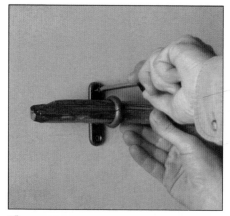

three *Screw the pipe holders to the wall. Attach the dowel in place. Hang the blankets over the dowel, with a 14-inch overlap to make a valance, pinning it in place with kilt pins.*

RENAISSANCE HEADBOARD

DRAMATIC EFFECTS HAVE BEEN used in this bedroom to create a very distinctive atmosphere, with the large painting dominating the room. It's a good idea to visit a museum store for the best range and quality of art posters—you are certain to find something for all tastes. You can apply a crackle-glaze or antiquing varnish to the poster if you want to create an authentically aged Renaissance look.

YOU WILL NEED

wallpaper paste

poster

medium-density fiberboard
(width x height of poster plus
mattress-to-floor
measurement), plus
allowance for frame

pencil

paste brush

ruler

picture rail molding (height
of poster x 2, plus width x 1)

mitering block

small saw

viridian green latex paint

paintbrushes

gold spray paint

fine-grade sandpaper

glue gun and glue sticks

crackle-glaze varnish

artist's red oil color

clean cloths

clear varnish

drill and fixtures to attach
fiberboard to bed frame
(depending on the type of bed)

one *Mix up the wallpaper paste. Mark the position of the poster on the fiberboard and apply paste to that section. Smooth the poster onto the board and let dry. Any air bubbles should disappear as the glue dries.*

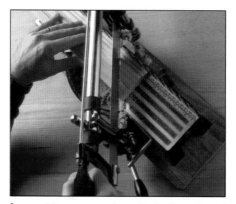

two *Measure and mark the lengths of molding for the frame. It goes along the top of the poster and down both sides to mattress height. Saw the corners on a mitering block. Paint a viridian green undercoat. Let dry.*

three *Protect your work surface, then spray a coat of gold spray paint over the green. Let dry. Rub the frame with fine-grade sandpaper, so that the gold is lifted on the highest ridges to reveal the green beneath. Do not overdo the sanding. Use a glue gun to stick the picture frame around the edges of the poster.*

four *Paint the whole surface of the poster with crackle-glaze varnish, following the manufacturer's instructions. Let the varnish crackle. Use a cloth to rub artist's oil color into the surface. Red is used here, but any strong or dark color will also work well. Rub the oil paint right into the cracks and cover the whole surface.*

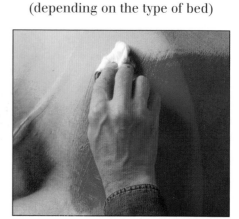

five *Rub the oil paint off the surface with a soft cloth. The color will stay in the cracks. Apply several coats of clear varnish to the poster. When dry, attach the headboard to the bed frame, using the drill and fixtures.*

CHAIRS AND TABLES

INTRODUCTION

TABLES AND CHAIRS ARE TWO OF THE MOST important elements in every home—they appear in most rooms and in many shapes and forms, from the elegant and luxurious to the everyday and useful. Everyone needs somewhere to sit and something to eat off. As they usually grace communal spaces such as kitchens or living rooms, they can suffer more from day to day living—from busy mealtimes, young children or family pets. They are also relatively quick to show wear and tear and very expensive to replace when they start to look a little ragged round the edges. So, if you are short on time, have a limited budget, and have more imagination than skill, we will provide simple solutions for instant, affordable and creative table and chair decoration ideas. This thrifty chic is also tremendously satisfying. Easy to follow, step-by-step photographs demonstrate how to paint, glue, tie, pin and staple a wide variety of materials, providing new looks for old favorites. Each project is self-contained and fully illustrated

Below: Wheat and bamboo trimmings turn a wooden chair into a Polynesian throne reminiscent of the South Seas. Place it in a sunny corner of your garden if you don't have a summer house.

with clear, step-by-step photographs designed for you to use at home.

Quite often, you will find that furniture needs little more than a new

cover or a decorative paint effect to give it a whole new lease on life,

so you certainly won't have to think of sacrificing every weekend

for months on end to take on a project. And by giving a bit of tender,

loving care to a flea market find—bought for next to nothing

and revamped equally inexpensively—you can create an individual

masterpiece of your own, giving your home a real sense of personal

style. So, flip through our wonderful and innovative ideas for paint

and fabric treatments and simple embellishments, then arm yourself

with a paintbrush or a staple gun ... and enjoy!

Above left: Napkins don't have to be white or plain. Embellish bold colors with flower shapes.

Above: Continue this plush fabric and rope treatment with matching tie-backs for curtains.

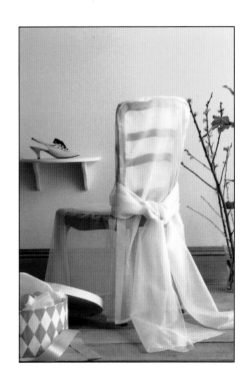

Right: See-through fabric draped over a chair turns the plainest bedroom into a boudoir. White fabric would reflect light back into a dressing-table mirror.

DRESSING FOR DINNER

FOR VERY SPECIAL OCCASIONS, why not dress up your table and chairs? Choose a style of corsage suited to the style of your chairs. A simple unvarnished country chair, for instance, calls for understated trimmings, whereas a fancy French one requires something much more elaborate. Trim the table to match. The individual flower arrangements can be given to your guests to take home. These ideas could not be simpler, but will add to the festivities.

YOU WILL NEED

florist's wire

silk or fresh flowers

fresh greenery

scissors

2½ yards organza ribbon and piece of organza

potpourri and star anises

fine string

glue gun and glue sticks

beads

A CHAIR WITH STYLE

one *Use florist's wire to join the flowers together at the stems. Silk flowers are best because they are bendable.*

two *Continue binding in flowers and greenery to make an attractive corsage. Trim the stems and tuck in any ends.*

three *Finish with a ribbon bow. Make a wire hook to attach the corsage to the chair.*

LIVENING UP THE TABLE

one *Fill a teapot with potpourri. Then cut a circle from organza, fill it with potpourri and tie the top with string. Twist a cinnamon stick into the tie and tie the bag to the lid.*

two *Make a bottle a necklace by pulling apart a piece of fine string into separate strands and gluing star anises to one strand.*

three *Decorate a decanter or jar with a piece of organza ribbon tied into bows, or threaded with beads.*

Pure Plastic

A PLASTIC TABLECLOTH is invaluable on a table that gets a lot of use—in a family breakfast room, for example—as it can be wiped clean in seconds and doesn't stain. As a rule, however, ready-made plastic cloths tend to be very plain or extremely garish. To make an attractive as well as practical cloth, why not cut a shaped trim from plain white plastic and make a simple design along the edge using a hole punch? Inexpensive, quick and very easy to make—what could be better? You could also make a matching cloth for a sideboard or serving area.

YOU WILL NEED
tape measure
plastic fabric
dressmaker's scissors
pencil
cardboard
hole punch
ribbon, string or rope
(optional)

one *Measure your table and cut the plastic fabric to the required size. Draw up and cut out a cardboard template for the scalloped edge. Draw lightly around the template on the wrong side of the plastic fabric with a pencil.*

two *Cut the edging shape with sharp dressmaker's scissors, keeping the scallops rounded and even.*

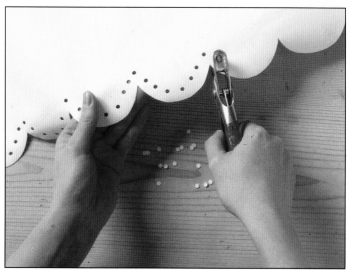

three *Punch out a design with a hole punch. You could thread ribbon, string or rope through the holes to add even more interest and, perhaps, a splash of color.*

TACTILE TABLECLOTH

ALL SORTS OF WONDERFUL TRIMMINGS are now available, and a trip around the notions department will, with a little imagination, generate any number of ideas. Here, simple upholsterer's webbing was used to edge a plain and practical burlap cloth. The webbing was decorated with string in very loose loops. The charm of this simple design lies in its interesting textures, so it is probably best to use materials in shades of the same colors, as here. However, if you wish, you could make a bold statement in bright primaries or contrasting colors.

YOU WILL NEED
about 2½ yards burlap
dressmaker's scissors
dressmaker's pins
needle and basting thread
iron
sewing machine
matching sewing thread
8¾ yards webbing
brown string

one *Cut the burlap to the size required, allowing for hems. Turn under the hems and pin, baste, press and machine-stitch. Cut a length of webbing to go around all four sides. Pin and machine-stitch the webbing around the edge.*

two *Lay the string on the length of webbing and twist it to experiment with different designs—a repeating pattern will look more professional.*

three *Pin, baste and hand-stitch the string to the webbing, to hold it securely. It doesn't matter if there are gaps in the stitching; the looseness of the string is all part of the effect.*

NEW WAYS WITH NAPKINS

NAPKINS IN JEWEL-BRIGHT colors add a wonderful and inexpensive splash of brilliance to any dining table and immediately conjure up visions of hotter climates and more exotic places. Choose tapestry yarn in strong colors to edge the napkins and trim each one in a different style, adding buttons and beads where appropriate. They will prove really eye-catching when used with a plain, boldly colored tablecloth, country-style china and chunky knives and forks.

YOU WILL NEED

colored linen napkins

colored tapestry yarn

tapestry needle

large button

about 50 tiny multicolored beads

tailor's chalk (optional)

one *If your napkin has an open-work edging, work a cross-stitch following the decorative holes in the edge. If not, work an evenly spaced cross-stitch along the edge. Attach a button with tapestry yarn at one corner.*

two *Work the edge of the second napkin in blanket-stitch by holding the thread under the needle and pulling the point of the needle through. Take a few strands of tapestry yarn, knot them in the center and stitch them to one corner.*

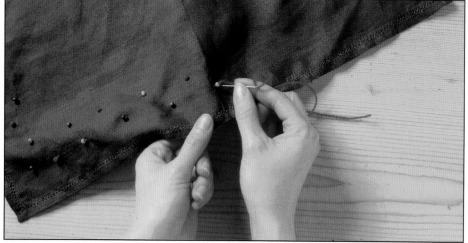

three *For the bead edging, work out a design by arranging the beads on a flat surface. You could mark these on the napkin first, by chalking tiny dots where you feel the beads should be. Sew the beads securely in place.*

four *Complete the edging with running stitch. Simply take the thread and weave it in and out of the fabric at regular intervals, to form a pretty line of stitches about ½ inch from the edge.*

EGYPTIAN TABLE-TOP

THE BEAUTY OF THIS TABLE-TOP design lies in its simplicity. Just one color was used on a bold blue background, with three similar images stamped in regimented rows. The table used here has a lower shelf, but the design would work equally well on most tables. The salmon pink prints show up well on the rich background, making it look even bluer. The stamps are pre-cut and are taken from Egyptian hieroglyphs. The finished table could be the surprising and eye-catching centerpiece of a room decorated in subdued colors.

YOU WILL NEED

3 hieroglyph rubber stamps

ruler and triangle

2 cardboard strips, one the length and one the width of the table, for position guides

felt-tipped pen

small paint roller

salmon pink latex or acrylic paint

piece of cardboard or plastic

one *Use the stamps and ruler to measure out the stamp positions. Place a cardboard strip along the edge of the table and mark as many stamp lengths as will fit along, leaving spaces between them. Mark stamp widths along the second cardboard strip.*

two *Place the cardboard strips at 90-degree angles to each other to mark the position of the first row. Coat the roller with paint on a piece of cardboard.*

three *Coat the hieroglyphs and stamp in sequence along the first row.*

four *Move the long strip up one stamp-space on the short strip, check that it is at 90 degrees and stamp a second row. Continue until the table is covered.*

FABRIC SWATHED CHAIR

THIS EFFECT IS STYLISH and practical and yet needs no sewing skills. None of the usual difficulties caused by the need for washing fitted covers apply, so you can capitalize on the sheer drama that is created by brilliant white. A generous quantity of fabric is the only essential; this project uses a king-size, pure cotton sheet, which is ready-hemmed, but you can use any wide, preferably washable, fabric that is soft enough to knot and tie. Why not consider this a stunning addition to your Christmas decor, by wrapping the dining chairs in red silk?

YOU WILL NEED

chair

fabric

sewing machine
(optional)

one *You need at least twice, and preferably three times, as much fabric as the width of your chair. Hem the fabric, if necessary. Throw the fabric over the chair and center it.*

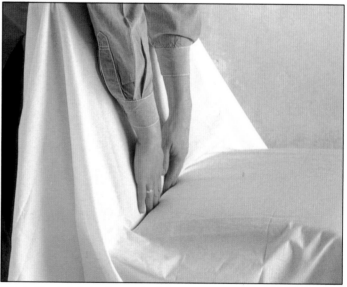

two *Tuck fabric down the back behind the seat of the chair. If the chair has arms, do this all around the seat, so that the cover doesn't pull when you sit on the chair.*

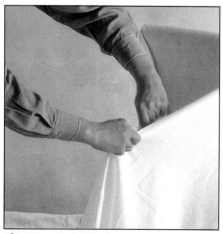

three *Sweep the fabric around to the back of the chair, letting it drape.*

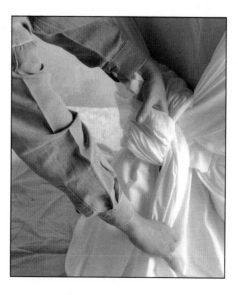

four *Tie a knot, making sure that the fabric is an even length on both sides and that you have attractive folds and drapes at the sides. Try to tie the knot confidently the first time; otherwise the fabric can look tortured and may be crumpled. Remember that the fabric should cascade down from the knot.*

ASTROTURF CHAIR

CLASSIC CONSERVATORY CHAIRS are usually made of expensive hardwood and are often rather boring and conventional in design. To create a truly modern garden room, therefore, why not jazz up a cheap fifties metal chair with strips of astroturf, available at garden centers and do-it-yourself stores. Complete the retro effect with some artificial flowers—although they are, as a rule, considered kitschy, their use is most definitely tongue-in-cheek here. The chair would also be an ideal conversation piece for a garden party.

YOU WILL NEED
metal chair

screwdriver

fine- and coarse-grade astroturf

staple gun

ruler

craft knife

glue gun

artificial flowers

one *Unscrew the seat pad and cut a piece of fine-grade astroturf to cover it. Staple it in place.*

two *Measure and cut strips of a coarser grade of astroturf and attach to the seat with a glue gun.*

three *Cut two matching pieces of coarse astroturf to fit over the central back struts of the chair. Glue the artificial flowers to the front piece.*

four *Fix both pieces over the struts with a glue gun.*

$\mathscr{S}$TOOL WITH WOOD

THIS IS A VERY SIMPLE and yet effective look, which does not involve any complicated techniques. A variety of wood moldings is available at your local lumberyard or hardware store, intended for embellishing doors and paneling. However, like the paneling used here, it also gives instant texture to otherwise plain objects, lending them unexpected style.

YOU WILL NEED

wooden stool

white undercoat paint, if necessary

paintbrushes

ruler

pencil

wooden moldings

glue gun

oil-based brown paint, mixed with 2 parts matte glaze (scumble)

creamy white oil paint

dry brush

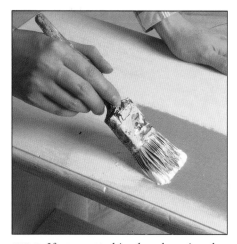

one *If your stool is already painted in strong colors, paint it white to give a neutral base color.*

‹ two *Draw a central grid in pencil on the sides of the stool and decide on the positioning of the moldings. Stick them onto the surface. Both curves and angles are suitable.*

three *Using the brown glaze and working continuously in one direction (to simulate the grain of the wood), paint the whole stool.*

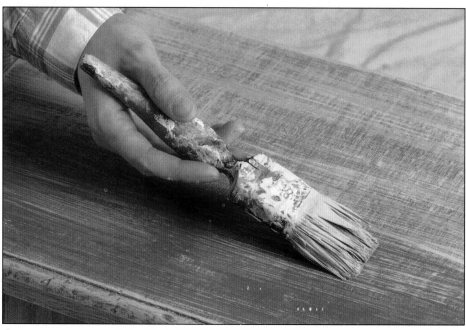

four *Using a pale wash of cream, paint over the moldings. With a dry brush, remove some of the glaze while still wet to give it a limed appearance.*

*M*AGIC CHAIR

COVERED IN NOVA SUEDE, this hard-backed chair has a split personality: It's a kitschy fifties dining chair by day and a theatrical throne in the evening. Throws are often used to cover easy chairs but the limitless possibilities of using them to add drama to a hard chair, totally changing its appearance, are often overlooked. Another advantage is that you can knot throws and tie them onto the uprights of a hard-backed chair, and extras, such as tassels or bindings, can easily be incorporated.

Any fabric that is wide enough is suitable for this treatment, but soft, textured fabrics, such as suede or velvet, are particularly stylish. Practicality is not an issue, because the covers can be whisked off to reveal the practical chair underneath.

YOU WILL NEED

hard-backed chair

large piece of plush fabric; for example, Nova suede

tassels or bindings
(optional)

one *Drape the fabric over the chair, making sure it touches the ground at the front.*

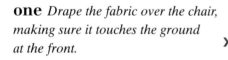

two *Take up some excess fabric from the back and form a knot over both chair pegs at the back of the chair.*

three *For further embellishment, secure the corners of the fabric with tassels or bindings.*

ROPE-BOUND CHAIR

COLONIAL-STYLE AND VERANDA CHAIRS have gained considerable popularity recently but, sadly, originals are extremely difficult to find. This is a good technique for a chair whose character would be lost if it were painted or stripped and yet which needs some form of embellishment. Natural trimmings, such as twine or burlap tape, can be expensive, as you will need about 90 yards. Look for less expensive forms of the same product, such as the thick rope used here. You could also use garden twine, clothesline or builder's scrim.

YOU WILL NEED
old chair
6 to 8 12-yard bales of
thick rope
glue gun

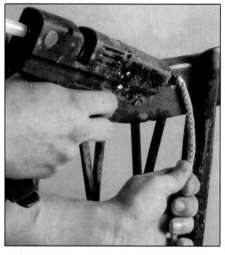

one *Starting at the back of the chair, secure the end of the rope with a small amount of glue from the gun.*

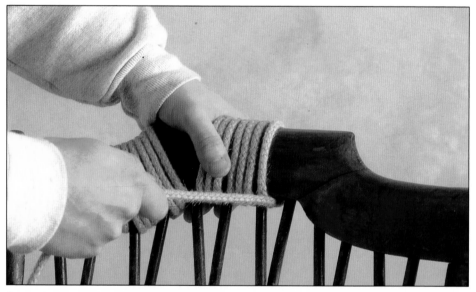

two *Begin wrapping the chair with rope, according to your chosen design.*

three *You can use two lengths at a time for the arms, starting with a slip knot.*

four *When you reach the end of the length, secure it by tucking it in at the back of the chair and then glue.*

SPACE-AGE CHAIRS

FOR AN OVERDOSE of the fantastic, create some space-age simplicity and make a statement that can't be ignored in your bathroom or kitchen. Vacuum-formed chairs appeared in vast numbers in our schools and offices as part of the sixties space-craze. A twenty-first-century update can be given to these forgotten and often discarded chairs by adding yet more space-age technology: Shiny silver space-blankets, used as emergency blankets. These are available at most camping stores and their silver appeal is unsurpassed. Vacuum-formed chairs themselves are the classics of their time and crying out for a facelift. Car spray paint is available in many colors, if you don't want silver.

YOU WILL NEED

2 plastic chairs

silver car spray paint

white glue

paintbrush

1 yard thin batting

1 yard of 54-inch iridescent lycra fabric

needle and strong thread

scissors

4 ping-pong balls

craft knife

space mat

china marker

space blanket

one *Spray the legs of the chairs silver. Apply a coat of white glue to the top and bottom of the first chair and stick on the batting.*

‹ two *Stretch the lycra tautly over the chair. Gather the fabric at the back and stitch it in place. Trim off any excess fabric and turn and baste to neaten the back. Cut holes in the ping-pong balls and insert a leg into each one.*

three *To line the circular hole in the second chair, use the china marker to draw the outline of the hole on the underside of the space mat.*

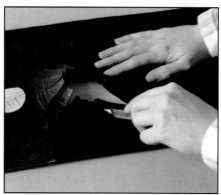

four *With a craft knife, cut a small circle from the center of the outline and then make straight cuts from the inner to the outer circle.*

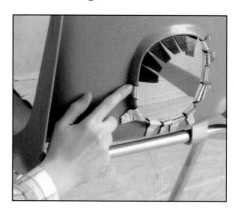

five *Apply white glue to the back of the chair and press the cut sections in place. Once the circle has been centered and the glue is tacky, apply the space blanket as a continuous strip.*

Sheer Fabric Chair

A BEAUTIFUL CHAIR with wonderful curved legs, a ladder back and cane seat might not seem to need further treatment; yet sometimes, for a change, or for a special occasion, such as a wedding party or a Valentine's Day dinner, you might want to decorate a chair without masking its integral beauty. A wistful, romantic appeal can be given by swathing the chair in translucent fabric to give it a softness that looks very special. The transparent fabric could be colored, or use one of the metallic fabrics in gold or silver, as long as the elements of the chair show through. Use the extra fabric to tie a sash in a knot or a big, soft bow and leave it either at the back or on the seat, like a cushion.

YOU WILL NEED

wooden chair

tissue or pattern-cutting paper

pencil

dressmaker's pins

3 yards of 54-inch transparent silk, voile or organza

fabric marker

dressmaker's scissors

measuring tape

sewing machine, matching thread and iron

one *On the paper, carefully trace the shape of the backrest of the chair. Use this as a template for cutting the back and front of the backrest cover, adding ¾ inch all around for seams. Pin the template to the fabric, draw around it and cut out the pieces. Trace the shape of the seat in the same way. Don't worry too much about getting an exact fit; the sash will take up any fullness. Transfer onto fabric, adding ¾ inch all around for seams.* >

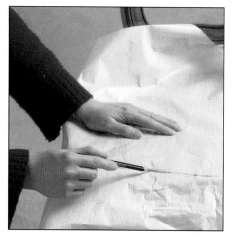

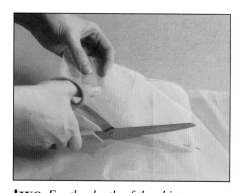

two *For the depth of the skirt, measure from the seat edge to the floor, then add ¾ inch for a seam allowance.*

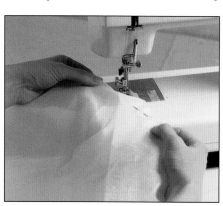

three *For the skirt, add 48 inches to the circumference of the chair seat. Cut as one panel. For the sash, allow 2 yards x 16 inches. Right sides facing, stitch the bottom of the front backrest panel to the top of the seat panel.*

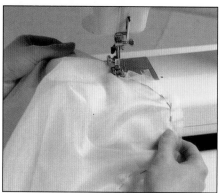

four *Press open all the seams as you go. With right sides together, stitch the front backrest panel to the back.*

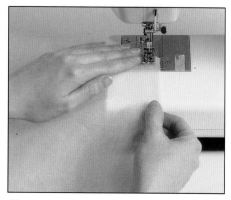

five *Hem bottom of skirt. Press, pin pleats. Hem top of skirt. Sew to seat panel at sides and front and to back panel at back. Fold sash in half, right sides together. Sew seams. Turn right sides out, stitch open end. Tie to chair.*

FUN-FUR CHROME CHAIR

ANOTHER COMMON flea market find is the chrome-framed chair. Suppliers of second-hand office furniture should have plenty of inexpensive examples. This one was found in very bad condition—the chrome was spotted with rust and the padding torn. The finished picture shows how even a really beat-up chair can be transformed into something chic. The fun-fur covering may seem a touch bizarre but, teamed with the chrome, it turns the chair into a unique furnishing. You need at least twice the length of each pad in fun fur.

YOU WILL NEED
chrome chair
screwdriver
chrome cleaner
soft cloth
craft knife
foam rubber or batting
staple gun
fun-fur fabric

one *Undo and reserve the screws and remove the old seat pads. Clean the chrome frame with chrome cleaner.*

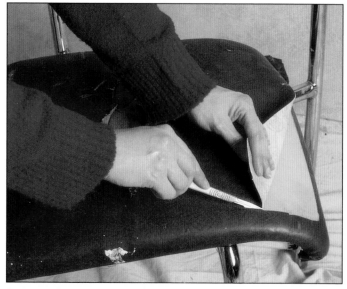

two *Cut away the old covering fabric and padding, to reveal the wooden base of the pads.*

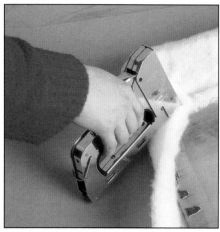

three *Cover the base and seat back with new foam rubber or batting, securing it with a staple gun. Replace the pads.*

four *Cover the pads with fun-fur fabric, using a staple gun to attach the fabric to the wood. Take into account the nap of the fabric, so it falls nicely over the curved edge. For the longest wear, the pile should run from back to front (i.e. it lies flat when smoothed in that direction). Fold the fabric over the chrome supports. Replace the screws.*

POLYNESIAN THRONE

A SPLENDID ADDITION to your conservatory or log-cabin-style summer house, this chair festooned with wheat and rushes is not destined to be a mere garden seat, but a haven for sitting and musing. Gardening has become an extremely popular pastime and garden centers are full of a huge variety of plants and garden paraphernalia. Customized garden furniture is much sought after and pricey, but you can make this stylish throne for very little money, with dried grasses, craft brushes, raffia, bamboo and rushes, which are available at garden centers or florists.

YOU WILL NEED
wooden chair
medium-grade sandpaper
oil-based brown paint
paintbrush
4 large bunches of wheat
large bunch of raffia
double-sided tape
craft rush brushes
saw
staple gun
dried bamboo and rushes

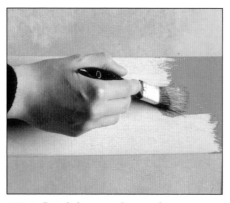

one *Sand the wooden surfaces to provide a key for the paint. Paint the chair with the brown paint to give it a wood-grain effect. You may find it easier to remove the seat.*

‹ two *Cover the horizontal strut of the backrest with a few lengths of wheat, tying them in place with raffia. Use the double-sided tape to hold the wheat while you work (the final attaching comes later). Attach two rush brushes diagonally by binding the stalks to the chair frame and at the crossing point with raffia. Shorten the two remaining rush brushes to the length of the vertical chair struts.*

three *To cover the verticals of the backrest, bind them with several strands of raffia. Slip stems of wheat through raffia until wood is covered. Tie two more brushes directly to front horizontals. Tie brushes to verticals.*

four *Bind the two side brushes with many strands of raffia. Discreetly part the brushes and secure them at the top with a few strengthening staples. Add decorative and reinforcing raffia in crisscross fashion to the back of the chair. Knot the raffia to secure it.*

five *Choose thin, flexible bamboo or rushes to bend over the top of the legs, staple in place, then bind with raffia. Staple a rough covering of wheat and rushes over the legs. As a final touch, and also to help it last, knot and crisscross more raffia between your turns.*

BUCKET STOOL

FLORIST'S BUCKETS in galvanized tin are widely available in a variety of heights; obviously, the taller they are, the better. Cover the metal seat pad in any fabric (a waffle-textured towel was used here). For a bathroom you could fill clear plastic fabric with foam chips or fun sponges. Dish cloths also make fun covers, and a layer of dried lavender would make a lovely scented seat.

YOU WILL NEED
1 yard heavy cord or rope
2 florist's buckets
glue gun
very large self-cover buttons
scraps of material for covering buttons
fabric-cutting tool for buttons
waffle-textured hand towel
large sewing needle and matching thread
circular cushion pad

‹ one *Attach the cord to the top rim of one of the buckets with the glue gun.*

two *Place this bucket inside the second bucket, applying glue to its rim, then invert both buckets.*

three *Use the fabric to cover the buttons as per the manufacturer's instructions.*

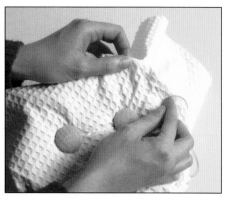

four *Sew the buttons to the center of the waffle-textured hand towel. Then use the towel to cover the cushion pad. Instead of smoothing out the gathering in the fabric, accentuate it, using the buttons as a focus. Glue the pad to the upturned bucket.*

CARDBOARD CHAIR

IT'S VERY IMPORTANT that you hunt down the correct cardboard of the heaviest weight direct from a cardboard manufacturer for this chair. An extra thick corrugated cardboard has been used here, resulting in a very sturdy piece of furniture. Remember that, as with wood, the vertical grain is the strongest. Cardboard furniture is particularly suitable for children because of their lighter weight. To hold your cardboard creation securely together, use gum arabic tape, as it is deceptively strong and therefore perfect for this project. The cardboard is left undecorated to create a minimalist look.

YOU WILL NEED

felt-tipped pen

metal ruler

4 sheets of very thick corrugated cardboard, 2 x 1½ yards

scissors

craft knife

self-healing cutting mat

gum arabic tape

4 thin dowels, pencils or chopsticks, 5 inches

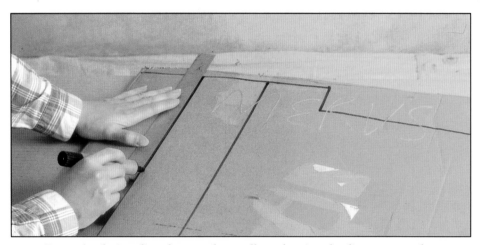

one *Draw the design directly onto the cardboard, using the diagrams on the next page as a guide. Make sure that you keep the grain of the cardboard running from the top of the chair to the bottom.*

two *Using the back of a pair of scissors and the metal ruler, score along the fold lines. Cut out all the shapes with a craft knife, then bind the edges with gum arabic tape.*

three *Assemble the chair in the same way as you would make a carton, folding and slotting the cardboard into itself. The backrest of the chair has flaps that fold into the arm rests.*

four *Slot the seat into position, making sure it is securely held in place. To give further support on the struts, insert pieces of dowel, or even pencils or chopsticks, through the cross-struts.*

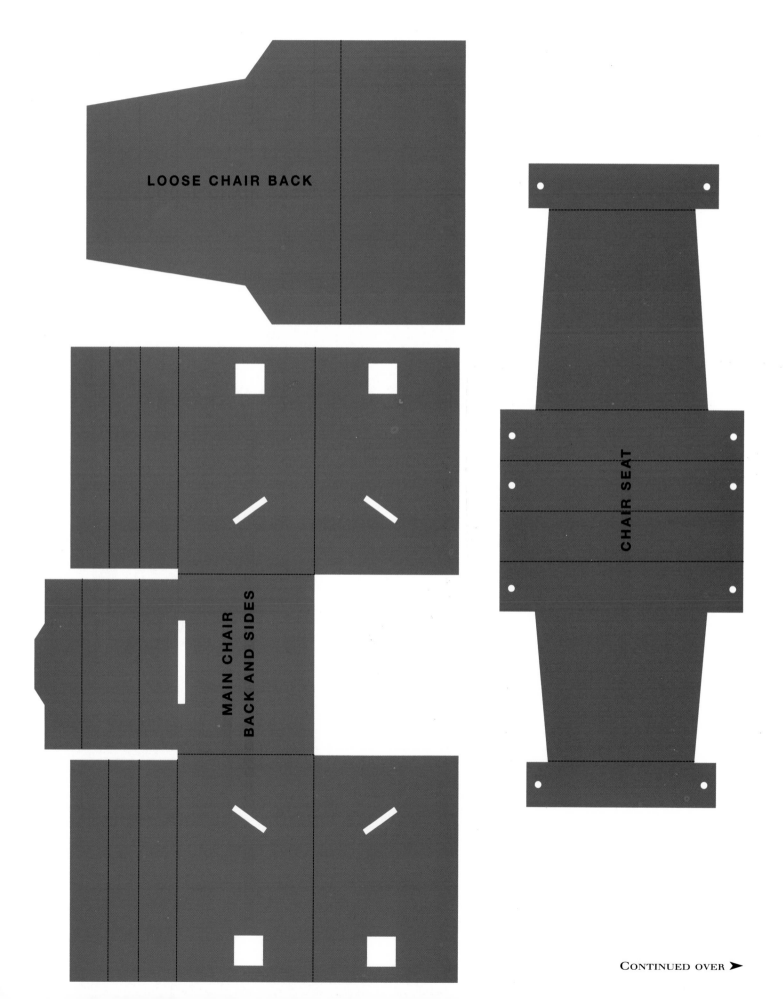

LOOSE CHAIR BACK

MAIN CHAIR
BACK AND SIDES

CHAIR SEAT

CONTINUED OVER ➤

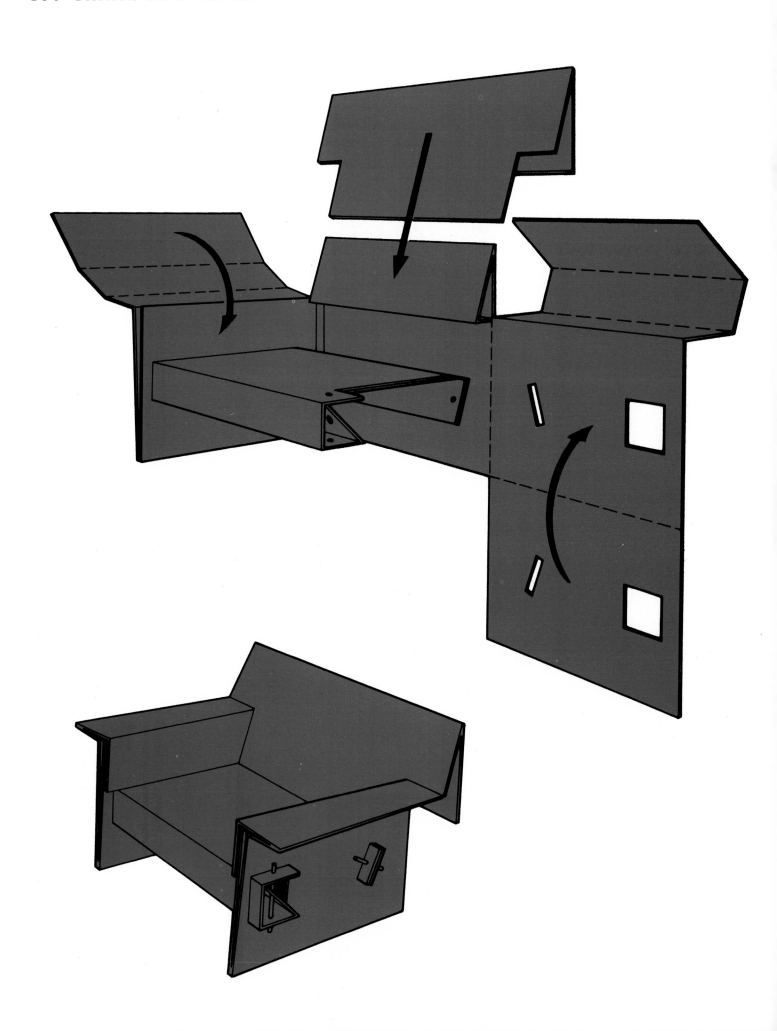

LIGHT AND SHADE

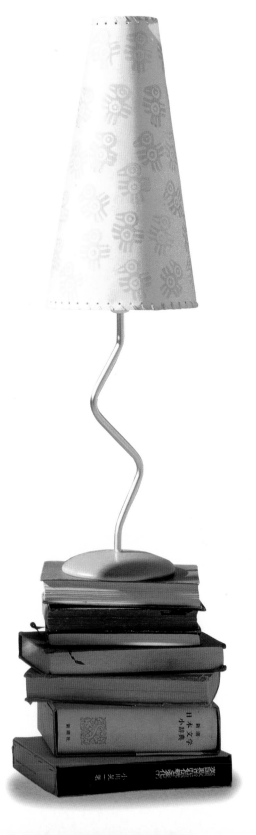

$\mathcal{I}$NTRODUCTION

THE LIGHTING IN ANY ROOM IS CRUCIAL—it has a huge impact on the overall atmosphere. You can use it to highlight the contours of a room, to attract attention to desirable features and to draw the eye away from less impressive corners. The options for interesting lights are endless, from high-tech spotlights to traditional standard lamps and classical sconces, and in this chapter, we have tried to explore plenty of alternatives. Simple, step-by-step photographs show how to transform everyday lampshades and bases by using interesting paint techniques, and embellishing them with raffia or covering them with beads. You can take a basic frame and cover it with tissue paper, or wrap it with crepe bandage, or create a lamp from bamboo—all the projects we have chosen are clearly photographed and provide a stunning gallery of different treatments for painting, adapting and decorating light fittings of all kinds. A good starting point is to look at the lights that are already in your home. Some of the quick projects could be just what is needed to give them an injection of style. Bases and shades can both be transformed with simple paint techniques or bead fringing, or stamped

*Left: The bird shapes stamped onto
this paper lampshade are inspired by
traditional Inca patterns.*

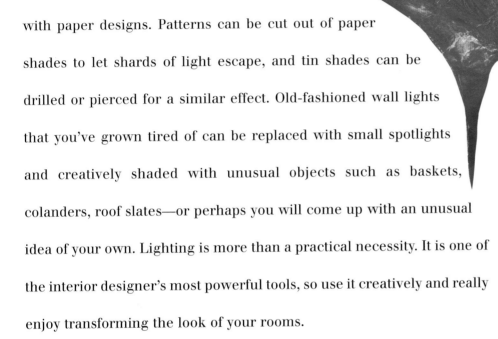

with paper designs. Patterns can be cut out of paper shades to let shards of light escape, and tin shades can be drilled or pierced for a similar effect. Old-fashioned wall lights that you've grown tired of can be replaced with small spotlights and creatively shaded with unusual objects such as baskets, colanders, roof slates—or perhaps you will come up with an unusual idea of your own. Lighting is more than a practical necessity. It is one of the interior designer's most powerful tools, so use it creatively and really enjoy transforming the look of your rooms.

Above: A pink paper lampshade is wonderfully frivolous and will cast a warm and comforting glow, just what you need as an antidote to the stresses of the world outside.

Below left: A light can, in itself, be an interesting object. Here, the conical shape complements decorative spears.

Below: Treat lampshades as blank canvases for your design ideas.

BENT-WIRE CHANDELIER

MAGICALLY CRAFTED FROM A roll of wire, this delicate little chandelier was twisted and curled into shape with long-nosed pliers. Making it is so much fun that you will probably want to make a pair. Bonsai-training wire, sold at garden centers and by bonsai-tree specialists, was used here. Hang the chandelier from a chain and hook so that it can twist and turn in passing air currents.

YOU WILL NEED

roll of silver bonsai-training wire

wire cutters

long-nosed pliers

roll of gardening wire

4 reinforced screws and screwdriver

glue gun with all-purpose glue sticks

4 thumb-tacks

4 nightlights

large sequins

one *Cut a 13¾-inch length of bonsai wire for the first kidney-shaped curl. Hold the wire with one hand, grip the end with the pliers and shape a curl. Holding the first curl in your hand, curl the other end. Make a single curl from a smaller piece of wire.*

two *Make two more single curls. Each branch is made of these four pieces. Cut a 4¾-inch length of gardening wire and bind the kidney-shaped curl and two of the single curls together, as shown. Wind the wire around neatly like a spring.*

three *Screw a self-tapping screw into the center of the binding, leaving at least ½ inch protruding at the top.*

four *Bind the third single curl onto the back of the kidney shape, winding a length of gardening wire into a neat binding as before. Snip off the end of the gardening wire at an angle, close to the binding. Repeat the above steps to make the four branches.*

five *Cut a 20-inch length of bonsai wire for the central column. Twist one end into a spiral and the other into a small hook. Make two small, tight curls and bind them into the top end of the column, facing inward. Bind the four branches onto the column.*

six *Apply a dot of glue to one of the screw heads and immediately sit a drawing pin on it, pointing upward. Repeat with the three remaining screw heads. Press a nightlight down onto each of the drawing pins. Thread the large sequins onto the curls.*

ANGULAR WALL LIGHT

THIS UNUSUAL WALL LIGHT IS a two-colored plastic shade slotted over a standard mini-spotlight. The two halves of the shade are simply clamped together with two shiny metal clips on each side. Before fitting the two pieces together, cut a hole in the back piece to slot over the base of the spotlight. Make the hole the same size as the spotlight base so that it fits snugly and will not slip. Place the back of the shade in position first, making sure that the bulb remains far enough from the plastic to avoid both accidents and damage to the shade.

YOU WILL NEED

brown wrapping paper

pencil

ruler and triangle

scissors

spray adhesive

sheet of yellow plastic

sheet of red plastic

craft knife and cutting mat

small halogen wall-light fixture

4 small metal clips

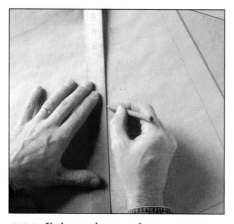

one *Enlarge the template on a photocopier. Transfer it twice to brown wrapping paper. Cut out the two patterns, leaving a ¾-inch seam allowance all around the edges.*

two *Spray the paper patterns with adhesive and stick one on each plastic sheet. Cut out the shapes and nick the ends of the fold lines, so that they will be obvious from both sides.*

three *Remove the paper, then score the fold lines, but be careful not to cut more than the surface. Practice on the scraps first to get the pressure right.*

four *Turn the sheets over and score the fold lines again, working between the nicks at each end. Fold up the shades. Cut a hole in the back shade to fit the spotlight base, place it over the spotlight, then attach the front piece with metal clips.*

PINK TISSUE SHADE

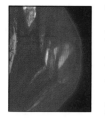

THIS BRILLIANT PINK PAPER lampshade will make a stunning centerpiece for a room and will cast a flattering pink light over everything—and everyone—at the same time. Make the size of the lampshade appropriate for your room. As it is very lightweight, it can be made quite big, which is useful if your house has high ceilings. Attach equal lengths of chain to the curled hooks and hang the light fitting in the center, so that the hot air rises out of the top of the shade.

YOU WILL NEED

bonsai-training wire

wire cutters

thinner wire

long-nosed pliers

chains to hang the shade

glue gun with all-purpose glue sticks

bright pink, good-quality tissue paper

water-based varnish

paintbrush

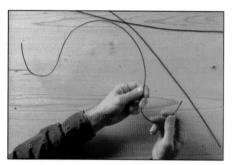

one *Cut three equal lengths of bonsai wire for the struts. Bend them into wavy shapes. You can exaggerate the shape, as the wire will spring back a little. Bind the ends together with thinner wire, using long-nosed pliers.*

‹ two *Attach a length of the thinner wire about 4¼ inches from the end of one strut, winding it around to secure it. Then take it around the other two struts in the same way. This will form the top of the framework. Wind around two more lengths of the thinner wire in the same way.*

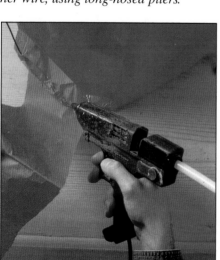

three *Using the pliers, curl the ends of the struts where the chains will be attached. Apply glue to one of the struts and fold the edge of a piece of tissue paper over it. Stretch the tissue across and glue it to the next strut.*

four *Continue in this way, overlapping where necessary, until the framework is covered. Wind and glue a strip around the point where the three struts are joined. Brush on a coat of varnish to tighten up the paper and bond the layers.*

ℰCCENTRIC CREPE

CREPE BANDAGE IS GREAT material to work with and makes a fun lampshade. It has just enough stretch to give a good tight fit, and the textured surface clings to itself as you layer the bandage. Keep an even tension as you wind it around a wire frame and use hot glue at key points, if necessary, to prevent any slipping or sagging. Make sure you leave an opening at the top to let the hot air escape.

YOU WILL NEED
copper bonsai-training wire

wire cutters

long-nosed pliers

thinner wire

glue gun with all-purpose glue sticks

rolls of bandage

one *Cut three equal lengths of bonsai-training wire and bend each into three curves, using the pliers. The wire will straighten up when you release it, so exaggerate the shapes as you bend them.*

two *Bind the three ends of the bonsai wire firmly together with the thinner wire. Be generous with the amount of wire because you need to make a solid fixture. Use the long-nosed pliers to help you to bind tightly.*

three *Run another length of wire between the three struts winding it tightly around each strut to form the lowest of three enclosing wires that will later provide the framework for the bandage binding.*

four *Wind around two more lengths of wire to complete the frame. Twist the ends of the struts into curved "feet."*

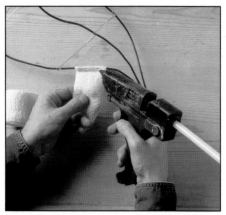

five *Glue the bandage to a strut about 2 inches from the binding at the top. Wrap tightly to secure. Wrap the bandage around the framework, pulling it to get the tension right. Apply glue whenever it crosses a strut.*

six *Wrap and glue a small length of bandage to cover the wire binding right at the top of the framework. Use the glue gun to seal the edge and be sure to leave a 2-inch gap around the top in order for the heat to escape.*

BIRD CAGE

ALREADY DECORATIVE AND DESIGNED to hang at eye level, birdcages need little adaptation to turn them into unusual Asian-style shades. This charming little wooden cage was made in the Far East. However, judging by the spacing of the bars, it cannot have been intended for keeping a real bird. Look for wooden or bamboo cages like this in gift stores, florist's or import stores and even at flea markets and yard sales (just make sure that they are in good condition). If necessary, adapt the steps to suit the shape of the cage. Hang the lampshade from a chain so that it can twist in passing air currents and use a low-watt bulb for safety.

YOU WILL NEED
small wooden or
bamboo birdcage
saw
wire cutters
tissue paper
pencil
scissors
ready-mixed wallpaper paste
paintbrush
pendant lamp fitting

one *Using a saw and a strong pair of wire cutters, cut off the struts that make up the base of the cage.*

two *Roll a sheet of tissue paper around the top section of the cage—here it is conical. Mark the shape in pencil.*

three *Cut out the shape. Apply wallpaper paste to the inside of the struts of the top section. Roll up the tissue paper, then unfold it inside the cage, pressing it against the pasted struts to form a lining. Trim away any excess.*

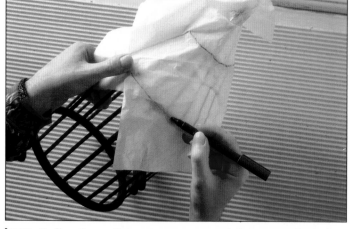

four *Cut out a rectangle of tissue paper to line the rest of the cage. Paste the inside of the struts, then place the tissue paper inside the cage, as before. Let dry. Ask an electrician to attach the pendant lamp fitting and to wire it to an electric switch.*

$\mathscr{C}$HICKEN-WIRE TORCH

THIS DRAMATIC SHADE WOULD look fabulous in an entrance hall or at the top of a staircase, especially if it is teamed with an interesting paint finish. The basic shape is a cone, but the shade's character relies on the layers of chicken wire interwoven with silver solder and copper wire. Spirals of wire, creating an unusual textural patchwork, hold the ragged, torn paper in place. The shade is hooked over a small halogen wall spotlight by means of a slit cut into the wire mesh. The light picks up the colors of the silver solder and the copper wire, adding another layer of brilliance on top of the grayish wire mesh, and shines through the different paper textures. The shade is very lightweight, but a coat of black latex applied to the base of the cone will add visual weight and create a feeling of substance and balance.

YOU WILL NEED

36 x 24 inches chicken wire

long-nosed pliers

hammer

wire cutters

small halogen wall-light fixture

silver solder

copper wire

3 different, highly textured natural-weave papers

black latex paint

paintbrush

screw and screwdriver

‹ one *Roll the chicken wire into a tube with a 6½-inch diameter. Using the pliers, pinch and twist the cut edges to make one end neat.*

two *Roll the tube into a cone shape, so that the unneatened end tapers down to a point. Pinch and twist the cut wire to hold the shape firm.*

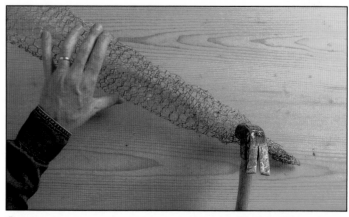

three *Compress the narrow end of the chicken-wire shape by hammering it on a hard surface. The wire mesh will scrunch up into a fairly solid mass.*

four *Use the wire cutters to make a slit in the back of the cone. This should be large enough to fit over the base of the wall-light fixture and let the cone lie flat against the wall.*

five *Cut two 20-inch lengths of solder and weave them in and out of the mesh. Follow the shape of the cone, spiraling the wire upward.*

six *Cut similar lengths of copper wire and weave them through the mesh. Here, a zigzag pattern is used.*

seven *Wind copper wire around the outside of the cone, "sewing" it through the mesh in places.*

eight *Add a patchwork of chicken-wire pieces. The different depths of wire will be picked out and enhanced by the light when it is switched on.*

nine *Tear up the three sheets of paper. The edges should be rough and ragged. Tear some pieces into strips and others into random shapes.*

CONTINUED OVER ➤

ten *Place the paper pieces randomly on the outside of the cone, and use spiraling strands of wire to bind them into place.*

eleven *Use the long-nosed pliers to tweak and pinch the paper in places, so that it becomes a part of the structure instead of just sitting on the outside.*

twelve *Carefully dry-brush black latex paint onto the narrow base of the torch to give a matte-black charcoal finish.*

thirteen *Fit the torch over the wall-light fixture. Bend the mesh so that it fits snugly around the base and put a screw in the wall near the top of the torch to hold it in place.*

Above: Chicken wire is cheap and surprisingly easy to work with. You can form the wire into elegant candleholders, candlesticks and shimmering bead domes.

ℒEADING LIGHTS

CHANGE YOUR SHADE and lamp base to something unique and quite sensational within the space of just an hour. Here, a basic shade was decorated with rough string threaded through punched holes. It is very easy to punch holes around the top and base of any shade, using a hole punch, and then thread through string, raffia, ribbon or yarn. To continue this idea, put small string bows at intervals around the shade and intersperse them with dried leaves.

YOU WILL NEED

lamp base and shade
hole punch
rough string
scissors
glue gun and glue sticks
dried leaves

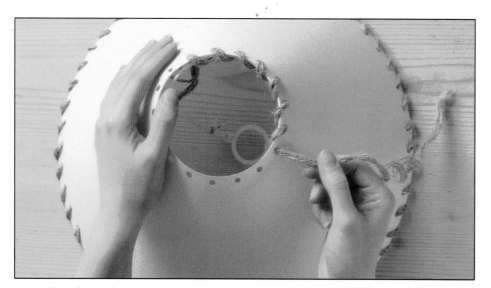

one *Punch evenly spaced holes around the top and bottom of the shade. Thread lengths of string through the holes, top and bottom.*

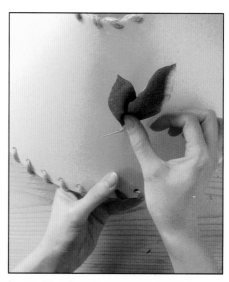

two *Use the glue gun to stick the leaves around the shade.*

three *Tie small string bows and glue them between the leaves.*

four *Put a line of glue down the back of the metal base. Starting from the top, bind a long length of string tightly around the stem. Use glue and a second length of string to cover the base. Press to make sure the string binding is absolutely firm. Make sure that the ends are glued securely in place.*

HANDMADE-PAPER GLOBE

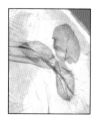

COVERING AN INFLATED BALLOON with papier-mâché may not be the most original creative technique, but old ideas are often the best ones. You could use a variety of different papers; here, light tissue paper has been mixed with fibrous handmade-paper scraps containing dried flower petals and leaves. Keep the same thickness across the top of the balloon, but let it taper off toward the tied end.

YOU WILL NEED

handmade-paper scraps
containing leaves and
flower petals
ready-mixed wallpaper paste
paintbrush
inflated balloon
cream or white tissue paper
gauze or mesh
pin
scissors
pendant lamp fitting
cardboard ring
all-purpose glue

one *Apply paste to small pieces of paper and stick them onto the balloon in a random overlapping arrangement, beginning at the top.*

two *Cover the top two-thirds of the balloon with three layers of paper, tissue paper and gauze or mesh. Set aside until bone-dry; this may take several days. Use a pin to burst the balloon and remove it from the shade.*

three *Cut a small hole in the top of the shade, using the lamp fitting as a guide to the right size.*

four *Reinforce the hole by gluing a cardboard ring inside the shade. Screw the two halves of the pendant lamp fitting together, one on either side of the shade, and ask an electrician to wire the fitting to an electrical cord.*

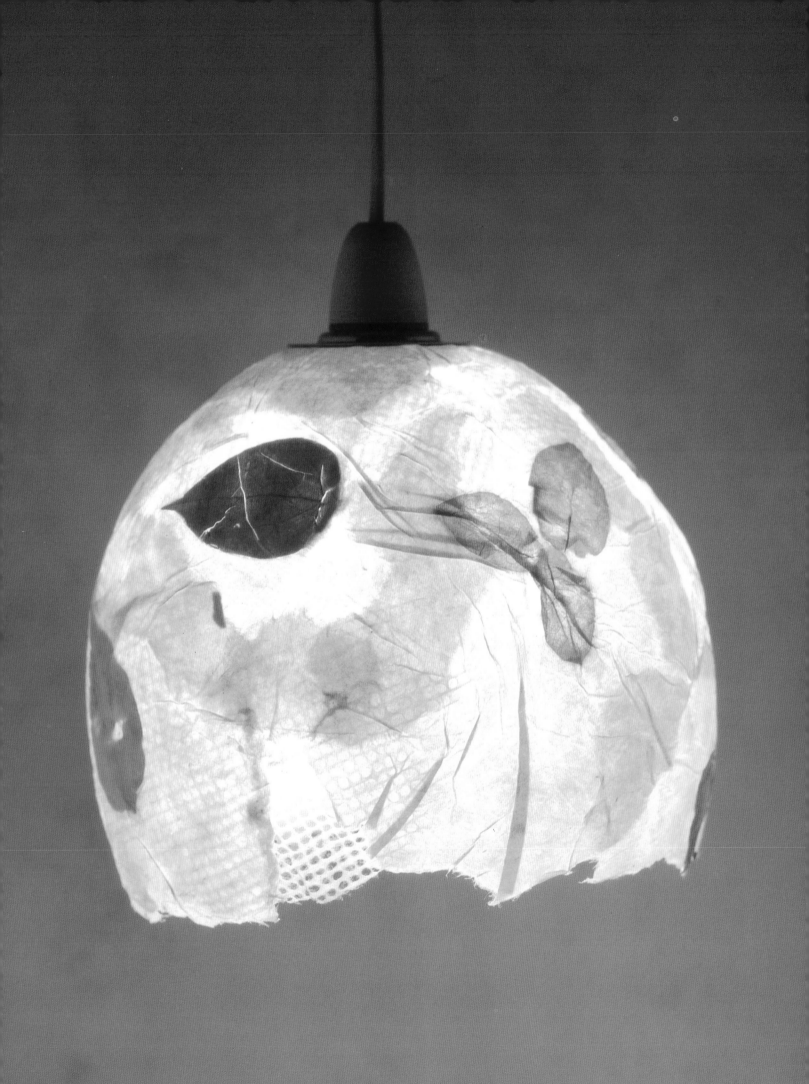

RAFFIA STANDARD

STANDARD LAMPS PROVIDE the perfect overhead light to read by without killing the atmosphere of a room as bright central ceiling lights often do. Placing one in the corner means that an individual can see what he or she is doing, while the rest of the room can be dimmed for watching television or general relaxation. Here, a turned-wood standard lamp has been enclosed in a sheath of raffia which is finished off by a "thatched" base that resembles a very clean chimney-sweep's brush.

YOU WILL NEED

turned-wood standard lamp

rubber bands

several bunches of natural-colored raffia

scissors

colored raffia

one *Place a rubber band at the base of the lamp pole, near the floor. Unravel the raffia and cut a handful of 15-inch lengths. Fold the lengths in half and tuck them under the band, so that it holds them in place just below the fold. Continue inserting folded lengths until the base is completely covered.*

two *Wind a strand of raffia around the rubber band several times and tie it tightly to hold the raffia base in place.*

three *Place a rubber band around the top of the lamp. Tuck bunches of raffia under it until the pole is covered. About 10 inches down from the band, wind a strand of raffia around the pole. Continue at intervals.*

four *At the base, tuck the raffia into the top of the base raffia, then bind to cover the seam. Trim any loose ends. Cover the plain raffia bindings with colored raffia.*

TRIMMED SHADE

TURN A RATHER BORING, plain-colored lampshade into a completely wacky extrovert by adding a dangling fringe of unusual trimmings. Almost anything non-perishable that will thread can be used—the brighter, the better. The choice is yours. Check out the toy store, particularly the inexpensive selection, where bright beads, miniature dolls and animals and fluorescent plastic balls are all waiting to be snapped up. Another good source is a stationery store; multicolored plastic paper clips can be put to a decorative use their inventors would never have imagined.

YOU WILL NEED

plain conical lampshade

square of paper or cardboard

pencil

triangle

hole punch

strong thread

needle

selection of beads, toys, baubles, etc.

glue (optional)

one *Place the lampshade on a square of paper or cardboard and draw around the bottom edge in pencil.*

two *Use a triangle to divide the circle into eight equal segments.*

three *Replace the shade on the paper or cardboard and mark the divisions around the edge in pencil.*

four *Use the hole punch to make eight small holes about ½ inch up from the edge of the shade, in line with the pencil marks.*

five *Attach a bead securely at the end of the length of thread, as an anchor, then thread on a selection of your chosen baubles and beads.*

six *Attach the thread to the shade by sewing it through one of the punched holes several times, then finishing with a secure knot. An extra bead can be glued to the edge of the shade to cover the thread. Decorate the rest of the shade in the same way.*

TRIO OF LAMPSHADES

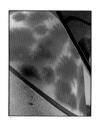

NOTHING COULD BE QUICKER, easier or cheaper than painting squiggles, spots or flecks of color on a few plain lampshades to add a touch of individuality to any room. The three shades shown here have each been made using a different decorative technique. All are fun to do, and only the black-and-white stripes require a steady hand. Use plain fabric shades and experiment with color, using it to reinforce an existing decorating theme or to add a spark of brilliance and give a quick face lift to a monotonous color scheme.

YOU WILL NEED

BLOTTING-PAPER EFFECT
plain fabric lampshade
paintbrushes
bright blue ready-mixed watercolor paint
droppered bottle

PAINTED-LINE EFFECT
cardboard
scalpel
cutting mat
metal ruler
plain fabric lampshade
black acrylic paint
paintbrushes: large square-tipped and small

FLECKED EFFECT
plain fabric lampshade
cardboard
pencil
scalpel
cutting mat
toothbrush
water-based acrylic, poster, watercolor or gouache paints: yellow ocher, brick-red and cream
paintbrush

BLOTTING-PAPER EFFECT

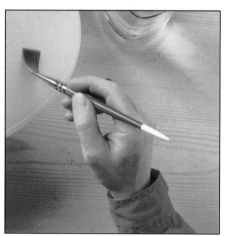

one *Dampen the whole outer surface of the fabric lampshade with water, using a paintbrush.*

two *Fill the droppered bottle with blue paint and squeeze it gently to leave one small drop on the shade. Watch the blot spread so that you can judge where to position the next drop.*

three *Turn the lampshade with your free hand and, as you do so, drop equal amounts of paint, spaced fairly evenly all around the shade.*

four *Fill the spaces between the blots with a more random pattern of differently sized dots, but be careful not to cover the original lampshade color completely.*

five *Holding the lampshade from the inside with your free hand and resting your painting hand on the work surface, paint the top and bottom rims solid blue.*

PAINTED-LINE EFFECT

one *Cut a right-angled piece of cardboard with one edge the same length as the height of the shade. Angle the other side to make it easy to hold.*

two *Hold the square-edged cardboard up against the shade and paint a wide squiggle to the right of it, using the large brush. After each squiggle, move the cardboard along; this will ensure that you paint vertically and don't slide off in one direction, which is very easily done when painting a shape like this.*

three *Paint fine squiggly lines between the fatter ones, using the small paintbrush. Support the wrist of your painting hand with your free hand to keep it steady.*

four *Finish off the lampshade by painting the top and bottom rims with a solid black line.*

CONTINUED OVER ➤

FLECKED EFFECT

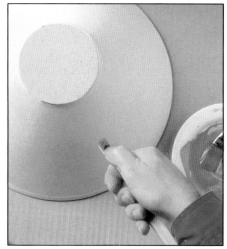

one *Place the shade upside down on the piece of cardboard and draw around the inside of the top rim. Cut this circle out, just slightly larger than the drawn pencil line, and place it on top of the shade to prevent any paint from dripping onto the inside.*

two *Place the shade on a protected work surface. Fill the toothbrush with the yellow ocher paint, then draw your thumb backward over the bristles to fleck the lampshade with color. Try to get a fine, even covering, but let the background show through.*

three *Clean the toothbrush, then dip it into the brick-red paint. Using the brush at an angle, make randomly placed wedge-shaped marks at different angles over the flecked pattern. Don't try for a regular pattern: Look at the example shown here to judge the effect you are after.*

four *To finish the decoration, clean the toothbrush, then apply the cream paint in the same way as the red. It may not show up much, but when the lamp is lit at night, all will be revealed.*

INCA BIRD PRINT

MAKE AN IMPRESSION on a tall conical lampshade by stamping it all over with a strong printed pattern. The shade used here is made of thin, mottled cardboard that resembles vellum in appearance and casts a warm glow when the lamp is lit. The stamp is based on an Inca bird design that is bold enough for a beginner to cut and is even enhanced by a slightly rough cutting style.

YOU WILL NEED
white paper
spray adhesive
high-density foam rubber
scalpel
white glue
flat plate
ready-made wallpaper paste
golden brown and darker brown ready-mixed watercolor paint in dropper bottle
small paint roller
conical paper lampshade

one *Photocopy the motif from this page. Spray the back of the copy lightly with adhesive and stick it onto the foam block. Cut around the shape with the scalpel and scoop away the background so that the motif stands out.*

two *Put a spoonful of white glue on the plate. Add a similar amount of wallpaper paste and a few drops of golden brown paint and mix well. Run the roller through the mixture to coat it evenly and use it to coat the stamp.*

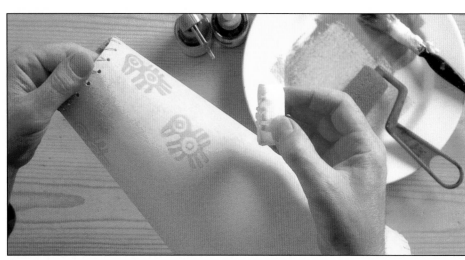

three *Print the bird motif on the lampshade by pressing the stamp onto the surface and then removing it directly. The wallpaper paste makes the paint gelatinous, leaving an interesting texture when you lift the stamp.*

four *Add a few drops of the darker paint to the mixture and stamp more motifs on the shade.*

STARRY NIGHT

CAPTURE A SMALL PIECE of the midnight sky by making this cut-out lampshade. Choose the deepest of blue shades, as the effect will be best if the light is completely blocked except by the star-shaped holes. The stars should be ½–¾ inch wide; any smaller or larger and the effect will be lost. Use a very sharp scalpel to cut the points of the stars, and always cut from the top of a point toward the middle. The lampshade looks spectacular at night, but you will get a similar effect by day with the decoration of raised metal stars. Available at notions stores, these have spikes at the back that are pressed through the shade and folded flat on the inside.

YOU WILL NEED
white paper
pencil
scissors
spray adhesive
navy blue paper lampshade
cutting mat
scalpel
metal-star studs
high-density foam rubber

one *Using the template, draw 50 stars on white paper. Cut the paper into small squares with one star in the center of each. Spray the backs of the squares with adhesive and stick them inside the shade. Arrange them randomly rather than spacing them in a pattern.*

two *Rest the shade on the cutting mat, and cut out the stars using a scalpel. Working from the right side of the shade, cut through any threads that remain and gently push the stars inward to remove them.*

three *Make sure that the spikes on the backs of the metal stars are all straight, otherwise they will not penetrate the shade. Hold a piece of dense foam rubber inside the shade to give you something to push against, then press the stars through and fold the spikes over at the back.*

GILDED PAPER PATCHWORK

GIVE TWO PLAIN LAMPSHADES a glittering new look by covering them in paper patchwork in two different styles. Although the techniques for each shade differ slightly, they have enough in common to be used as a stunning pair. The paper can be any type that is not too thick: newsprint, tissue paper, brown wrapping paper, photocopied typescript, sheet music or fine woven paper. Make a feature of ragged edges and avoid a regular, neat finish. The very special finishing touch is added with flashes of brilliant gold. The leaf used here is called Dutch metal. It is applied in the same way as gold leaf but costs much less. If you have never done any gilding before, these shades are a good starting point.

YOU WILL NEED

CUT-PAPER PATCHWORK

selection of interesting paper materials: corrugated cardboard, colored scrim ribbon, brown wrapping paper, handmade papers, paper mesh

scissors

plain cream fabric or paper lampshade

ready-made wallpaper paste or white glue

household paintbrushes for applying glue, an artist's paintbrush and a firm-bristled brush

gold size

Dutch metal leaf

soft cloth

TORN-PAPER PATCHWORK

selection of interesting paper materials: photocopied typescript, paper mesh, brown wrapping paper, handmade fiber paper, handmade paper, tracing paper

shellac

household paintbrushes for applying stains and glue, and an artist's paintbrush

turpentine

water-based stain: a natural wood shade

plain cream paper lampshade

ready-made wallpaper paste or white glue

gold size

Dutch metal leaf

soft cloth

CUT-PAPER PATCHWORK

one *Cut out "squares" from the different materials. Make them roughly equally sized, but trim them at an angle on both sides to taper slightly to fit the shade's conical shape.*

two *Try various combinations of texture and color until you are happy with the arrangement. Apply a coat of wallpaper paste or white glue to the backs of the shapes and stick them in place on the shade. Make sure the edges meet in order to form a solid patchwork.*

three *Paint "stitches" of gold size to link the squares together. Think of patchwork stitching, and make the lines vertical on the top and bottom and horizontal on the sides.*

four *Cut the Dutch metal leaf into strips, still on the backing sheet. Gently press the leaf onto the tacky gold size.*

five *Use a firm-bristled brush to clean away all the excess leaf, leaving just the stitches. Burnish with a soft cloth.*

TORN-PAPER PATCHWORK

one *Tear the different papers into similarly sized shapes, leaving the edges ragged and uneven.*

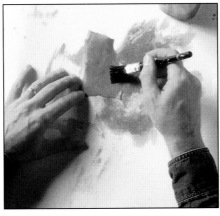

two *Tint one-third of the shapes with shellac. It is fast-drying and will make the papers stiffer and also slightly transparent. The brush will need cleaning with turpentine.*

three *Tint another third of the paper shapes using water-based stain and let them dry.*

four *Arrange the shapes on the shade, overlapping them in places and making a feature of the ragged edges. Practice with different arrangements until you are happy with the result.*

five *Apply wallpaper paste or white glue to the backs of the shapes and stick them onto the shade, using the stained shapes first. Space them wide apart to start and build up gradually.*

six *Fill in the gaps with the untinted torn papers.*

CONTINUED OVER ➤

seven *Paint a neat ½-inch borderline all around the top and bottom of the lamp-shade with gold size.*

eight *Cut the sheets of Dutch metal leaf into strips, leaving the backing sheet still in place.*

nine *Press the strips against the tacky gold size along both edges. Overlap them when you need to; the leaf will only stick to the sized sections.*

ten *Finally, rub off any excess metal leaf and burnish the entire design to a shine with a soft cloth.*

ASIAN SHADE

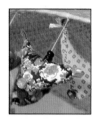

THE GLOBAL SUPERMARKET is now well and truly a part of our lives, and strings of brightly colored fabric birds from Asia have become as familiar to us as imports from closer to home. The lampshade made here is a combination of Chinese bamboo weaving and Indian textile work, put together in a way that is reminiscent of an Australian bush hat. The lampshade looks best when hung low over a kitchen table or anywhere that needs light combined with vibrant color.

YOU WILL NEED
string of Indian hanging textile birds

scissors

needle

embroidery floss

assorted beads

bamboo lampshade

scrap-paper measuring strip

one *Cut the retaining bead off the string of hanging birds, and remove the cord to separate the birds and beads.*

two *Thread the needle with about 12 inches of embroidery floss and tie a bead at the end of the floss. Push the needle up through the existing hole in one of the birds, and then thread on three more beads.*

three *Attach the bird to the shade, letting it hang down three finger-widths from the rim. Divide the rim into ten equal sections and attach a bird at each division.*

four *Attach an inner row of birds one-third of the way up the shade. Position them so that they hang between the birds on the outer row and at a slightly higher level. Use a paper measuring strip to calculate the floss lengths required.*

STAINED-GLASS BULB

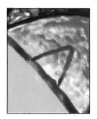

LIGHT BULBS CAN BE PAINTED in jewel-like colors to look like little illuminated stained-glass balls and create an unusual and impressive conversation piece. Ordinary light bulbs can be used, but the one shown here is a large 60-watt decorative globe bulb. Painted bulbs deserve to be shown off, so hang them low over a table, with a shallow shade that will not distract attention from the pretty patterns cast by the colored shapes. Special glass paints are available at art and craft stores. You don't need to buy much, as a little paint will go a long way.

YOU WILL NEED

waterproof marker

3 pieces of cardboard

light bulb

scalpel and cutting mat

strip of corrugated cardboard

sticky tape

glass paints: pink, green, yellow, blue and black

paintbrushes

one *Draw a circle on each piece of cardboard: one the size of the widest part of the bulb, one the size of the center of the star design and the third in between the two. Cut out the circles. Slip each piece of cardboard in turn over the bulb and draw a guideline on the glass where each sits. Carefully draw the guidelines for the rest of the design.* ❯

two *Roll up the corrugated cardboard strip to make a base for supporting the bulb. Secure the roll with sticky tape.*

three *Begin painting the top of the bulb. Start with the central dot and radiating arms of the star. Support your painting hand with your free hand to steady it.*

four *Working carefully, fill in all the different parts of the design, applying more than one coat where necessary to build up the color. Let the paint dry, then paint a thick black line around each color section to give a stained-glass effect.*

Woody Nightshade

WOOD VENEER IS A THIN SHEET shaved from a seasoned tree trunk and is sold by timber merchants who supply furniture makers. Each sheet is unique, so choose the veneer with the best grain; it will look even better with light shining through it. The lampshade shown here is made from flamed-ash veneer. The veneer hangs from a simple wooden frame but you could use a square picture frame (without the glass). Carefully remove one edge of the frame, thread on curtain rings and glue the piece back. Suspend the veneer from the frame using clipped curtain rings. Hang the lampshade on cord or leather thongs from a ceiling hook, with a pendant lamp fitting and bulb dangling inside it.

YOU WILL NEED

4 equal lengths of wooden dowel, mitered

glue gun with all-purpose glue sticks

curtain rings with clip attachments

metal ruler

scalpel

sheet of wood veneer

4 equal lengths of cord or leather thongs

‹ one *Attach three pieces of dowel using the glue gun. Thread the rings onto the frame before gluing the last piece of dowel in place.*

two *Measure the width of one side of the frame and, using the scalpel, cut four strips of veneer, one for each side. Make the length roughly twice the width; for a natural look the pieces should not be precisely the same size.*

three *To finish, attach two clips to each sheet of veneer, then tie a cord or thong to each corner for hanging.*

CONTAINERS

INTRODUCTION

CONTAINER DECORATING PROVIDES highly imaginative and innovative projects for transforming old containers or creating new ones in quick, simple, stylish and beautiful ways. Put an end to cluttered shelves and overcrowded closets, protect your belongings from dust, spills or breakage and find exciting ways to jazz up your home. If you've always thought of containers as mere practical objects in which to store anything from flowers to cookies, then you will be amazed at how cheap, everyday items can be easily made over into chic containers, bringing a personal dash of style into every room in your house. Take old paint tins, jam jars, bottles, bags, baskets or shoe boxes and give them a whole new lease on life by converting them into plant pots, shoe racks or funky chests of drawers—cover them with fabric, perhaps, or glue on buttons, beads or shells ... there are no limits to what you can do. The projects we show you can serve as a rich source of ideas to help you add a variety of colors, textures, patterns and shapes to whatever style of organization you opt for. Whichever project you

Below: Choose containers with interesting shapes, such as the bottles pictured, then all you need to do is emphasize their basic forms by adding texture to surfaces.

choose to make, you can simply use our

suggestions as a springboard for your

own creativity, so don't be afraid to modify or

embellish once your confidence has grown. Adapt ideas

and techniques to suit your own style and existing decor. An afternoon

spent sticking and gluing is totally absorbing, and at the end of the day

you will have a wonderful sense of achievement, too. All the techniques

used here are clearly photographed for each project and are designed to

be easy to follow. Throw inhibition to the wind and enjoy creating great-

looking effects at next to no cost.

Above: Favorite footwear deserves the very best of care, so fashion a suitably stylish resting place.

Below left: Gilded boxes are easy to make but create a luxurious mood.

Below right: Make paper boxes to fit any size using origami techniques.

String Bottles

Liqueur bottles have such attractive shapes that it seems a shame to put them into the recycling bin. This method of recycling enables you to continue enjoying them even after you have enjoyed their contents. The bottles used here are sherry, crème de menthe and Armagnac. This project is very easy to do and it can almost seem like therapy once you've gathered together a ball of string, some glue, a pair of scissors and three interestingly shaped bottles. Make yourself comfortable, put on some relaxing music and start winding the string around the bottles.

YOU WILL NEED

ball of thick string

glue gun with all-purpose glue sticks (or all-purpose glue)

3 interestingly shaped bottles

scissors

one *Coil one end of the string around like a coaster to make a base. Place a dot of glue in the center of the bottle base. Heat the glue gun and apply glue in spokes over the base. Press the string onto them. Draw a ring of glue around the edge to make the base secure.*

two *Circle the bottle with the string, working your way up and applying sufficient glue as you go. Make sure you get a good bonding on the bends and curves.*

three *When you reach the top of the bottle, cut the end of the string and apply plenty of glue to it so the finish is neat with no fraying. Repeat these steps with the other bottles.*

FANCIFUL SHOE BOX

IF YOU ARE ONE of those people who always takes the shoe box home with new shoes, only to throw it away reluctantly a while later, then this is the project for you. Your instincts to take the box in the first place are right, as shoe boxes are the perfect shape and size to make useful containers. This box is covered with brown wrapping paper—yet more good recycling—that was rolled and twisted, then unraveled and stuck onto the box to provide an interesting textured surface. The "bark" is made from torn strips of white paper, coated with wood stain to give a streaky finish. The end result is a unique, natural-looking container suitable for anything from potpourri to an index card system.

YOU WILL NEED

shoe box

cream latex paint

paintbrushes

brown wrapping paper

pre-mixed wallpaper paste and cheap brush

scissors

white glue

thick white paper

wood stain (such as antique pine)

thick, coarse string

square of calico, 4 x 4 inches

clips or pegs

glue gun with all-purpose glue sticks (or all-purpose glue)

one *Paint the shoe box with cream paint until all of the lettering is completely covered. Let dry.*

two *Roll up some brown paper, crumpling it. Fold up, then twist it as small as possible. Untwist and open it out.*

three *Apply a coat of wallpaper paste to the box. Place the box centrally on the brown paper.*

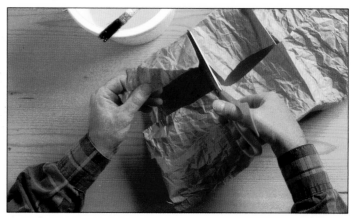

four *Fold the brown paper around the box, pressing it into the pasted surface, but not smoothing it too much. Pinch the paper along the edges of the box and cut along these. Fold the end flaps inside, sticking them in place with wallpaper paste.*

five *Fold the brown paper around the sides of the box, one end at a time, pasting one on top of the other to create two large triangular shapes.*

six *Fold the triangular shapes up over the sides and paste them against the inside of the box.*

seven *Neaten the inside by cutting a piece of brown paper to fit the base exactly. Paste it over the paper edges.*

eight *Using a dry brush, paint a streaky coat of undiluted white glue on the white paper. Leave some areas of the paper unpainted to let the wood stain show through. Let dry completely.*

nine *Brush wood stain onto the white paper. It will be resisted by the white glue where it is at its thickest and part-resisted in other places. This creates the bark effect.*

ten *Tear the paper into rough triangular shapes. If you tear at a slight angle, the paper will rip through its thickness and make the edges white and thin. Paint these white edges with wood stain so that they blend in.*

CONTINUED OVER ➤

eleven *Roll up the paper triangles, beginning with the widest part and rolling toward the point. Bundle the strips together with string and tie a reef knot. Separate the strands of string so that they bush out from the knot.*

twelve *Fray the edges of the calico piece, then scrunch it up in the middle, using clips or pegs to hold the shape. Heat the glue gun and apply glue to the scrunched folds. Press the calico onto the center of the box lid.*

thirteen *Remove the clips or pegs from the calico and apply more hot glue. Press the bark bundle on top of the calico.*

fourteen *If you are using the box to store index cards, write labeling on some spare "bark" paper and glue it to one end of the box.*

$\mathcal{B}$LANKET CHEST

YOU CAN ALMOST GUARANTEE that every interesting pine chest has been discovered by now, stripped and sold for a profit, but there are still plain, solid work-chests around that can be used as a good base for this project. The blanket used for covering the chest is the utilitarian sort used by furniture moving companies as a protective wrapping. Any blanket would be suitable, but this sort has lots of "give" because of the way it is woven and so can be stretched for a smooth fit. The chest has a piece of upholstery foam on it so it doubles as a comfortable bedroom seat. The lid is held down by a leather strap—suitcase straps or old horse tack are ideal as they come in longer lengths than leather belts.

YOU WILL NEED
wooden chest
screwdriver
pliers
tape measure
blanket
dressmaker's scissors
staple gun
upholstery foam rubber, to fit lid
ruler
cutting board
craft knife
leather strap
upholstery tacks
small hammer
scrap cardboard

one *Unscrew and remove the hinges from the lid and remove any protruding nails or screws. Measure around the chest for the length of the blanket. Then measure the height of the chest. Double the height and add 5 inches.*

‹ two *Cut the blanket to size. Spread it out, and lay the chest on its side in the middle with an even amount of blanket on either side and 3 inches below the base. Cut from the front edge of the blanket, in a straight line, to the left and right front corners of the chest. Staple the cut section inside the chest.*

three *Smooth the blanket down the side and staple it under the base. Cover the rest of the chest in the same way. Fold the blanket around from both sides to meet at the back and staple it in place. Staple all the lining neatly inside.*

four *Cut a piece of blanket about 4 inches larger than the lid on all sides. Place the foam in the middle of the blanket with the wooden lid on top. Press down the foam, pull up the blanket on one side and staple it in place.*

five *Cut a triangular section off each corner. Leave enough blanket to fold up and staple to the lid. Fold the cut edge up and staple it across the corner.*

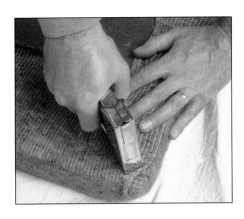

‹ **six** *Staple the side pieces over the first. Neaten by folding and trimming. Work on diagonal corners alternately.*

seven *Trim the chest and secure the fastening strap to the lower half with upholstery tacks. Use a cardboard strip as a guide to keep the spacing even.* ›

BUTTON BOX

BUTTON BOXES are an old-fashioned delight that should not be allowed to disappear altogether. There was a time when most homes had a cookie tin filled with an assortment of buttons for sewing and knitting projects. You can make your own button box to store these little treasures. The wooden box used here is an empty tea container with a sliding lid, covered with black felt and decorated with buttons.

YOU WILL NEED

wooden box with sliding or hinged lid

black latex paint

paintbrush

black felt

chalk

dressmaker's scissors

rubber-based fabric glue

craft knife

cutting board

buttons

glue gun with all-purpose glue sticks
(or all-purpose glue)

one *Paint the box black, inside and out. Let dry. Put it on the felt and draw in chalk the shapes needed to cover it: a rectangle for the base and long sides up to the grooves for the lid; a strip to cover the two ends and the base a second time; and a strip for the lid, stopping short of the runners.*

two *Cut out the felt pieces. Then spread fabric glue onto the base and sides of the box and smooth the shorter strip of felt onto it. The felt will stretch a bit at this stage. Spread a thin strip of fabric glue along the top edge of the sides and fold the felt over it. Let it dry completely.*

three *Trim off any edges for a neat finish. Glue the longer strip of felt onto the base and up both of the ends in the same way. Trim off any excess. Cover the lid with felt, then begin arranging the buttons to make an attractive design.*

four *When you are happy with the design, use the glue gun to stick the buttons in place. The glue will set immediately, so work quickly and place the buttons accurately. Decorate the sides of the box with stripes of colored buttons.*

five *Glue a row of white and pearl buttons along the top edge of the sides to complete the design.*

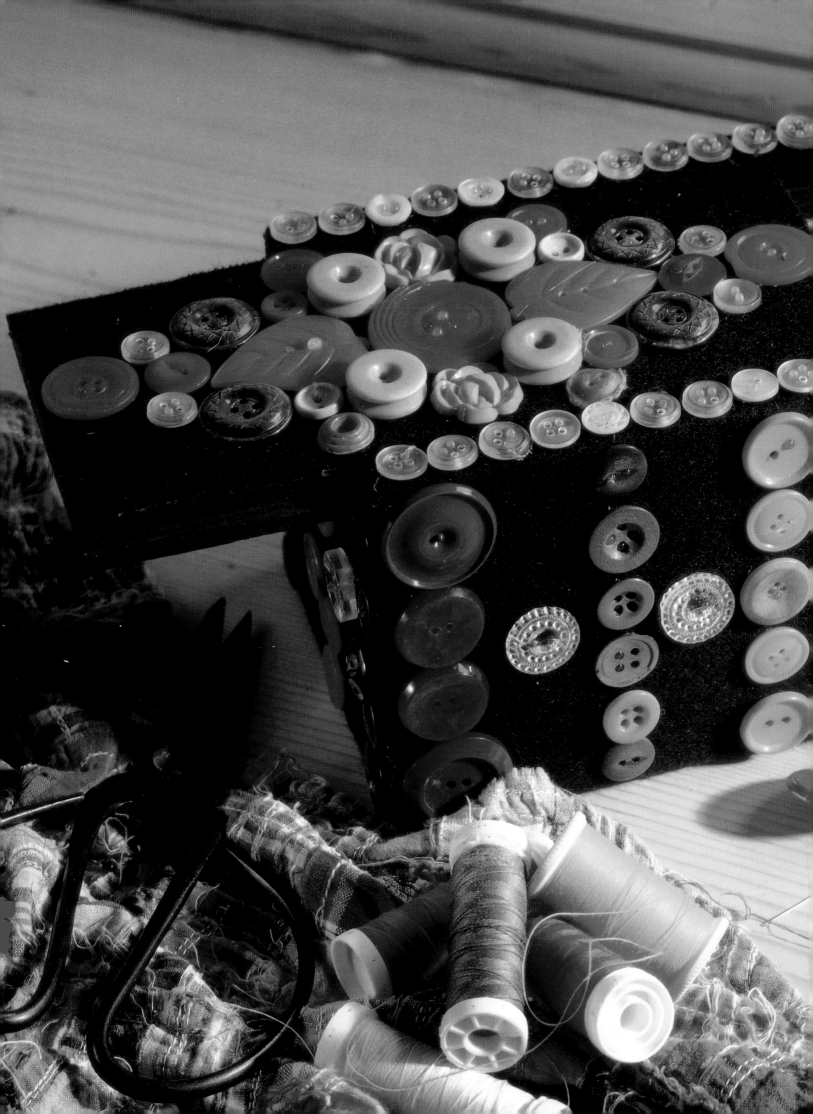

STAR CUPBOARD

THIS ATTRACTIVE LITTLE cupboard fits in the moment you have finished it. While its style is individual, it does not scream out for attention, and it has that comfortable, lived-in look. It was painted, stamped, then painted again and, finally, given a coat of antiquing varnish, then rubbed back in places with a cloth. It glows from all the attention and took just one afternoon to make. This style of decoration is so simple that you might consider transforming other furniture in the same way.

YOU WILL NEED

wooden cupboard

latex paint (olive green, off-white and vermilion)

scalpel

kitchen sponge

white glue

matte varnish (antique pine)

dish cloth

one *Paint the cupboard with a coat of olive green latex. While the paint is drying, use the scalpel to cut the sponge into a star shape.*

two *Pour some off-white latex onto a plate. Dip the sponge star into the paint and print stars all over the cupboard. Let dry.*

three *Make a mixture of two-thirds vermilion paint and one-third white glue and coat the cupboard liberally.*

four *Finish with a coat of tinted varnish, then use a cloth to rub some of the varnish off each star.*

Lizard-Skin Boxes

THESE SMART ANGULAR BOXES look crisp and exclusive, but they are, in fact, no more than paper-covered foam-core board. They make great containers for jewelry, barrettes or cufflinks, and they would add a touch of elegance to any desk or dressing table. When you make your own boxes, there are no manufacturing constraints, so you can make them any shape you like, however unconventional. Foam-core board is light and easy to cut and glue. Buy it at art and craft stores, and buy lizard-skin paper at specialty paper stores.

YOU WILL NEED

foam-core board

cutting board

felt-tipped pen

ruler

craft knife

glue gun with all-purpose glue sticks (or all-purpose glue)

3 different lizard-skin papers

spray adhesive

one *Place the foam board on a cutting board and mark a four-sided angular shape for the base. Cut out the shape. Measure each side, then decide on the height of your box. Cut out four rectangular side sections to fit those measurements. Heat the glue gun and run a thin strip of glue along each base edge, then stick the sides on. The glue will set right away, so work quickly and accurately.*

two *Place the box on a sheet of foam board and draw around it. Add 1¼-1½ inches all around for the lid overlap. Cut this out. Do this again, taking off ½ inch all around, for the lower half of the lid. Glue the two lid sections together. Cut a strip of lizard-skin paper wide enough to line the inside and outside of the box and to fold underneath. Apply spray adhesive to the paper, then wrap it around the box.*

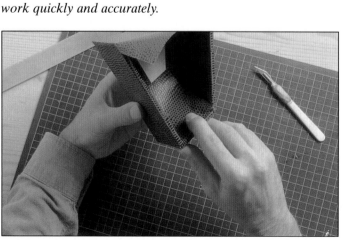

three *Cut down into the corners and fold the paper inside the box. Do the same underneath, smoothing the paper flat onto the box. Apply more glue where necessary.*

four *Cut out paper to cover lid. Glue in place and cut corners. Cut two identical shapes for a handle and glue together. Cover the handle with paper and glue to the top of the box.*

MOSES BASKET

THESE GENEROUS-SIZED WOVEN BASKETS were originally designed as easy, convenient and comfortable transport for young babies. Sadly, these old-fashioned cradles do not conform to stringent modern safety regulations, so present-day newborns have safer, but rather less charming, plastic and metal contraptions instead. Moses baskets are not completely obsolete, however. They are used here as fresh and airy hanging containers for clothes and also provide an attractive decorative feature for a bathroom or bedroom. Alternatively, you could use them for easy toy storage in a child's nursery.

YOU WILL NEED

plank of wood

tape measure

saw

sandpaper

drill, with wood and masonry bits

1 long or 2 short branches (or poles)

penknife (or wood carving knife)

dowels (optional)

2 Moses baskets

wood glue

hammer

plastic anchors and screws

screwdriver

one *Cut two squares of wood at least 4¾ x 4¾ inches and 2 inches deep. Sandpaper the edges and drill a hole through the middle of each square, slightly smaller than the diameter of the branches. Carve away the branch ends so that they fit tightly into the holes. Sandpaper them slightly.*

two *Use dowels or scraps from the branches for the pegs. Taper the ends.*

three *Measure the distance across the basket between the basket handles and drill two holes the same distance apart on top of each branch. Apply wood glue to each branch and tap them into each square.*

four *Apply wood glue to the peg ends and fit them into each branch. To attach the top branch to the wall, drill holes in the four corners of the square of wood, and four corresponding holes in the wall. Using the plastic anchors and screws, screw the branch to the wall. Attach the lower branch to the wall allowing about 4 inches of clearance between the two baskets.*

PRETTY POTS

MINIATURE TOPIARY WILL LOOK both eye-catching and charming on a windowsill or collected on a table, but don't forget to make the most of their containers. Terra-cotta pots have their own special appeal, but can also be treated to a variety of embellishments, from tassels to tape. Subtle, natural colors are best as they look best with the pots themselves and with the small pebbles used to conceal the florist's foam.

YOU WILL NEED

florist's dry foam block

sharp knife

3 old terra-cotta pots

2 straight twigs

glue gun and glue sticks

2 florist's dry foam balls

fresh foliage, such as box

selection of pebbles

curtain weight

fine string

string tassels

masking tape

craft knife

self-healing cutting mat

matte varnish

paintbrush

one *Cut the florist's foam block in half and cut each block to fit into two of the pots. Position the foam in the pots. Insert the twigs and then glue them in place, to act as the stems of the trees. Glue the foam balls on top.*

two *Cut small pieces of foliage to the required size and insert them at random in the foam balls, to create a casual, carefree effect.*

three *Cover the foam in the pots with a layer of small pebbles so that it is completely concealed.*

four *Thread the curtain weight onto string and tie it around one of the pots. Decorate the other pots with tassels or designs cut from masking tape with a craft knife. Varnish to make the masking tape secure.*

ALL BOXED UP

THERE IS A HUGE VARIETY of boxes available, ranging from plain and simple white wooden boxes to shoe boxes to oval trinket boxes. Make a set of three using easily available natural materials. Boxes can be trimmed with almost anything you want: bottle caps, paper clips, string, rope or a collage of stamps. Linen tape (used in upholstery) is available at notions departments.

YOU WILL NEED

plain wooden box
tape measure
scissors
linen tape
needle
matching sewing thread
2 wooden beads
glue gun and glue sticks
twig
small slatted wooden box
small package of potpourri
small Shaker-style box
dried leaves and fir cones

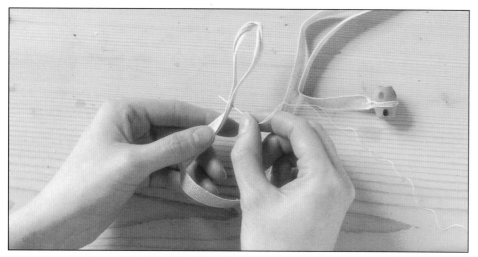

one *Measure the plain wooden box. Allow an extra ¾ inch at one end for the bead and about 3 inches for the loop. Cut two lengths of linen tape to this length. Sew a loop in the end of each tape and attach the wooden beads to be used as toggles.*

two *Secure the tape to one end of the box with glue, leaving the toggle and loop free so the lid can be opened. Repeat on the other side. Glue a twig to the top of the lid, as a decorative "handle."*

three *For the slatted wooden box, sort through the potpourri and choose the items you would like to use. Glue them to the lid. Glue the dried leaves and cones to the Shaker box, and glue linen tape around the sides.*

ORIGAMI BOXES

ORIGAMI IS THE JAPANESE ART of paper-folding where the most extraordinary three-dimensional objects are made from a single folded square of paper. This little box is a suitable project for a beginner, but it may take a couple of practice attempts before it suddenly "clicks." You can make the boxes any size you like, and use any paper that is not too flimsy. Wrapping paper is good as it creases well and is cheap and strong.

YOU WILL NEED

sheet of paper

scissors

double-sided tape
(this breaks all the rules!)

selection of paper squares
for practice (optional)

one *Fold and trim a sheet of paper to make a perfect square. Fold the square corner to corner. Open it to show the creases of four equal triangles. Turn it over and fold into four square quarters. Unfold it so you can see the creases of eight equal triangles. The center of the paper is Point A.*

two *Hold the model in the air and push all the sides together so that the corners meet in the middle. Flatten the model. Point A is now a corner of the flattened model. Keep it facing you.*

three *Fold the point opposite Point A over to meet it. Crease it along the mid-line. Now fold it back up to the mid-line and crease the fold. Unfold it again. Fold the same point up to the last crease, then fold it over again, up to the mid-line. Turn the model over and repeat this step.*

four *With Point A still facing you, take the top layer of the left-hand corner and fold it over onto the right-hand corner. You are now faced with a square. Fold the left-hand corner and the top layer of the right-hand corner into the center point, and crease. Bring the right-hand top layer over onto the left. Turn over and repeat.*

five *Point A now forms the base of a smaller triangle. Fold this up at the point where it meets the sides. Crease, fold it in the other direction and crease. Unfold. Insert your hand and splay your fingers while pushing up the bottom of the model, Point A. Fold down the two pointed sides level with the others and tuck the ends under. Secure with a small piece of tape.*

All the Trimmings

CHOOSE THE CHEERFUL PRIMARY colors of blue and red and team them with white for a crisp, clean look with a slightly nautical feel. You can also trim black with white for classic appeal or use several shades of one color to add a subtle lift. Felt is an easy, lovely and inexpensive way to trim plain fabrics, whether on shoe bags, linen bags, throws or cushions. You can add as much or as little decoration as you choose.

YOU WILL NEED

round template

2 squares of red felt, about 8 x 8 inches

2 squares of blue felt, about 8 x 8 inches

fabric marker

pinking shears

dressmaker's pins

blue cord

needle and matching sewing thread

string

fabric item, such as a shoe bag or quilt

one *Find a round template: It could be a can lid, coin or anything similar. Place the template on the felt and draw around the template with a fabric marker. Cut around the circle with pinking shears.*

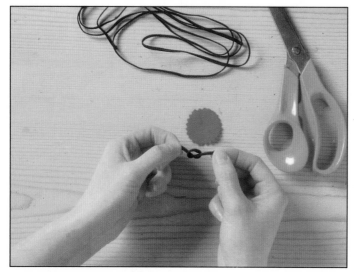

two *Pin two circles together, knot short lengths of cord and sew them onto the circles.*

three *Repeat with lengths of string. Sew the circles onto your shoe bag, quilt or other fabric items.*

News on Shoes

SPECIAL SHOES DESERVE a home of their own, and these sturdy wooden wine boxes can be made stylish enough to house anything from sturdy boots to Cinderella's glass slippers. The boxes were lined with different types of newsprint, which were layered and stuck down like papier-mâché. Select your newsprint to suit your shoes—put leather lace-ups in the pink financial pages, party shoes in comic strips and velvet pumps in the arts and literary pages.

YOU WILL NEED

wooden wine crates

sandpaper

white glue

paintbrushes

variety of newsprint

craft knife

clear matte varnish
(or shellac)

one *Sand down one of the wine crates. Then mix white glue with water (50:50) and apply a coat to the inside.*

two *Apply another coat of the glue mixture, then smooth newsprint over the inside. Apply undiluted white glue along the top edges and smooth the paper over it. Let dry before applying more paper and glue at random.*

three *Let dry, then trim the paper along the outside top edges with a craft knife. Varnish the whole box with either clear matte varnish or, if you want an "aged" look, shellac. Let dry, then re-coat at least twice.*

GILDED BOXES

THE RE IS NO PAINT or spray that gives a finish to compare with gold leaf, or its cheaper counterpart, Dutch metal leaf. It glows and glitters and can be burnished with a soft cloth to leave a gleaming surface. The art of gilding is surrounded by mystique because it requires a great deal of skill to lay the fragile sheets of gold leaf onto gold size or glue. This design was created using a kit suitable for beginners, which can be bought at art and craft suppliers. The flat surface of the box makes it easy to apply, but it is important to follow the manufacturer's instructions, as the drying time is crucial to the success of the project.

YOU WILL NEED

design tracing or photocopy

spray adhesive

high-density foam rubber

craft knife

round painted wooden box
with lid

fine-grade sandpaper

pencil

gold leaf kit

paintbrush

plate

small foam roller

cotton balls

fine steel wool (optional)

one *Select a suitable design or motif from a source book, and photocopy or trace to size. Spray the back of the design with adhesive and stick it onto a block of foam rubber.*

two *Carefully cut out the design, starting in the middle. Then cut around the outside.*

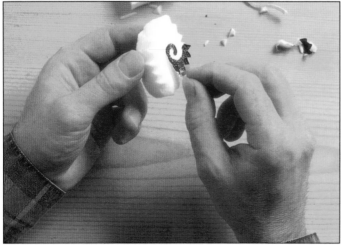

three *Once the cutting is complete, carefully peel off the paper pattern.*

four *Rub the entire surface of the painted box lightly with fine-grade sandpaper to make a rough surface for applying the gold size.*

six *Carefully paint a strip of gold size between the edge of the box lid and the pencil line and also around the top and bottom edges of the lid sides.*

five *Draw a pencil line around the top edge of the lid. Use your fingers to keep the line an even distance from the edge.*

seven *Put some size on a plate and run the roller through it until it is evenly coated. Using the roller, coat the foam stamp thoroughly and evenly.*

eight *Stamp an even pattern around the side of the box, re-coating the stamp after each print. Stamp four shapes inside the lid border line and one in the center.*

ten *Holding the lid at an angle, apply the sheets of gold leaf around the sides in the same way.*

nine *Leave the size until it has the right degree of "tack" (according to the manufacturer's instructions), then invert the lid onto a sheet of gold leaf. Smooth the gold leaf over the edges so that it is in contact with all of the size.*

CONTINUED OVER ➤

eleven *Rub the surface with cotton balls. All the "un-sized" gold will flake off, leaving the design behind.*

twelve *If the brand new gleaming design overwhelms you, rub the box lightly with steel wool to create an antiqued look.*

PUNCHED-METAL BUCKET

THE IDEA OF DECORATING metal objects with raised punched patterns has been around ever since sheet metal was invented about 300 years ago. Silver is probably best-known for this decorative treatment, but cheaper metals can also look very impressive. Bare metal buckets are ideal for this sort of pattern-making, and all you need is a pen to draw your guidelines and a hammer and blunt nail for the punching. You can practice your technique on any tin can to find the ideal sort of tap needed to make a good bump without piercing the metal.

YOU WILL NEED

bare metal bucket

felt-tipped pen
(not water-based)

blunt nail
(or center punch)

hammer

rag

lighter fuel
(or similar solvent)

one *Draw your pattern on the inside of the bucket. These motifs come from South America, but any repeated curves or angles are suitable.*

two *Rest the bucket on a piece of wood to protect your work surface. Tap the nail with a hammer, keeping the dents regularly spaced. About ½ inch is fine.*

three *Continue hammering the pattern all over the inside of the metal bucket.*

four *Use a rag and lighter fuel to clean off the pen pattern that is left between the punched marks.*

CIRCULAR PAINTED BOXES

THIS PROJECT EXPERIMENTS with three different paint effects. The first, rust, looks especially good when used on a material that doesn't naturally rust, such as wood. Verdigris is a natural substance that forms on the surface of weathered brass and is a beautiful turquoise-green color. The third finish used here is crackle-glaze, which looks a bit like lizard skin. This is the most time-consuming of the three paint effects because of the drying time needed between coats.

YOU WILL NEED

3 wooden boxes, with lids

water-based paints: dark gray, 2 shades of rust, green-gray, stone, 2 shades of green and maize yellow (according to required finish)

handful of fine sand

plate

paintbrushes

3 foam sponges

clear matte varnish, crackle-glaze base varnish, crackle-glaze varnish

alizarin crimson oil paint

2 rags

turpentine

THE RUST FINISH

one *Mix sand into the dark gray base coat for texture. Apply two coats of paint to the box. Let dry. Dab on the darker rust color with a sponge. Cover most of the background.*

two *Dab on the lighter rust color. If you are in any doubt about how it should look, find some real rust and copy it. Finally dab in just a touch of green-gray. Do not overdo this as it should blend in rather than stand out as a sharp contrast.*

THE VERDIGRIS FINISH

Paint the box with the stone base coat color. Dab on the lighter green with a sponge. Cover most of the background with this. Dab on the other green using a sponge. Apply a coat of clear matte varnish to protect the surface.

THE CRACKLE-GLAZE FINISH

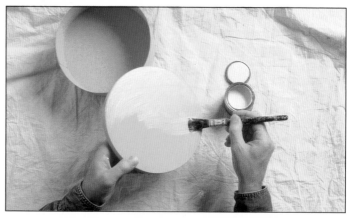

Paint a yellow base coat and a coat of crackle-glaze base varnish. When dry, apply a coat of crackle-glaze varnish. Let dry. Rub crimson oil paint into cracks with a rag. Dip a rag in turpentine; rub the surface so red paint remains in the cracks.

CAMEMBERT NUMBERS

THIS PROJECT SHOULD be linked to a wine and cheese party or the befriending of a French restaurateur, as it involves nine Camembert boxes. It is always a relief to be able to recycle packaging, and these empty boxes are certainly given a new lease on life in the form of a stylish set of containers. Enlarge the numbers on a photocopier so they fit your boxes, and cut them out as stencils. If you find the task too daunting, trace the numbers onto the boxes and paint them in.

YOU WILL NEED

9 Camembert boxes

fine-grade sandpaper

clear matte acrylic varnish

number templates

craft knife

cutting board

spray adhesive

stenciling plastic or waxed stencil cardboard

enamel paint: 9 colors plus silver

paintbrushes: medium, stenciling, fine-pointed and square-tipped

compass and pencil (optional)

shellac button polish

one *Remove any paper labels from the boxes. Rub the wood with sandpaper to get rid of any rough edges. Apply a coat of clear matte acrylic varnish to all the boxes.*

two *Take the templates, or make your own, and enlarge them on a photocopier so the numbers are 3 inches high (or fit within a border of about ½ inch). Cut out each one.*

three *Stick the photocopies onto the stencil material with spray adhesive. Stick them underneath stenciling plastic, but on top of stenciling cardboard. Cut out, making the incisions away from the corners.*

four *Stencil a number on each lid in different colors. With a fine-pointed brush, paint a band about ½ inch wide around each lid. (If necessary, use a compass). With a square-tipped brush, paint a band of silver around the edges. When dry, rub them down lightly and apply shellac.*

Snowflake Storage Jars

ALMOST EVERY KITCHEN COULD USE a face-lift every now and then. Rather than pay exorbitant prices for a completely new look, why not just cheer up your storage jars, simply and inexpensively, and give your kitchen a breath of fresh air? You can create a whole new atmosphere and a really individual look, by stamping patterns on your jars with acrylic enamel paint. The finish is quite hard-wearing and is tough enough to stand up to occasional gentle washing, but take note that it will not withstand the dishwasher.

YOU WILL NEED
pencil
tracing paper
spray adhesive
upholstery foam rubber
scalpel
dish cloth
glass storage jars
white acrylic enamel paint
plate
tile

one *Trace your chosen pattern shape, lightly spray it with adhesive and place it on the foam rubber. Cut around the outline with a scalpel. Cut horizontally into the foam rubber to meet the outline cuts and remove excess foam rubber.*

two *Clean and dry the glass jars. Spread a coating of paint onto a plate and make a test print on a tile to remove excess paint from the stamp.*

three *Holding the jar steady, press the stamp around the side of the jar.*

four *Rotate the stamp 90 degrees and make the second print directly below the first. Continue in this way, alternating the angle of the print.*

INDEX

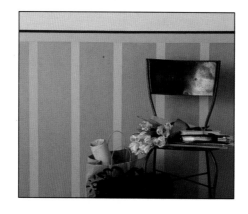